KV-050-221

Snorkelling and Skindiving

An introduction

Horace E. Dobbs

Oxford Illustrated Press Limited 1976

The Author

This book is dedicated to the founders of the British Sub-Aqua Club without whose efforts the author might never have enjoyed countless hours of excitement and pleasure underwater.

CONTENTS

Unless otherwise stated, all the photographs in this book were taken by the author using a Nikonos camera.

© Oxford Illustrated Press Ltd. and Horace E. Dobbs 1976

Set in 9/10pt Univers medium by Parchments, Oxford Printed and bound in Great Britain by Chapel River Press, Andover, Hants.

Oxford Illustrated Press Ltd., Shelley Close, Headington, Oxford.

ISBN 0 902280 37 6

Foreword by
H.R.H. The Prince of Wales

PRESIDENT OF THE BRITISH SUB-AQUA CLUB

It is probably true to say that Dr. Dobbs is one of the best known figures in the British diving world today and for the past four years has achieved the amazing feat of being elected to the British Sub-Aqua Club Council with the highest number of votes. He is therefore eminently well-qualified to produce this excellent and most readable of introductions to snorkelling and skindiving.

I must admit that I have always been rather intrigued by the kind of activities which offer an element of danger and excitement to the participant. The challenge is often irresistible and I can well understand the enthusiasm engendered by such sports as snorkelling and skindiving — but they can be lethal pastimes if, as Dr. Dobbs says, the basic rules are ignored and sensible precautions neglected. Two golden rules are firstly, never go diving on your own and, secondly, always make sure someone is left in the boat.

There is a unique fascination about the underwater world which is impossible to explain to those who have not experienced this new dimension. Occasionally it is frightening and eerie. When I first began to explore underwater I swam around in small circles, anxiously looking behind me to see if I was being followed! However, familiarity with the element brings a greater awareness of submarine life as it goes on about you — particularly if you go diving with an experienced person who inspires confidence and is the source of useful advice.

One of Dr. Dobbs' great talents is his ability to explain often difficult subjects in simple terms and I am sure that this book will fire many people's imagination and encourage them to explore another dimension of our existence, which in turn is a step along the road to discovering the real secrets of life.

Charles.

The First Skindivers

How did the word skindiving come about?

It was first used during the early days of the development of the sport of underwater swimming to differentiate it from other diving activities. There were the professional divers who were known as 'copper nobs' or 'hard hats'. These names were derived from the copper helmets they wore to which were attached tubes and lines that went to the surface. They wore rubberised canvas suits and plodded over the seabed in cumbersome lead-soled boots. Then there were the high divers who performed aerobatics before plunging into the water: when one of the pioneer skindivers said he was going diving his friends were likely to ask 'how high?' not 'how deep?', on the assumption that he was referring to diving from a board. The pioneers of the sport of underwater swimming used a pair of watertight goggles and dived literally 'in the skin' wearing just a pair of swimming trunks, so they were called 'skindivers'.

Since those early days the sport of underwater swimming has advanced at a rapid pace. The aqualung was introduced. The aqualung provided the underwater swimmer with a supply of air that enabled him to stay down for long periods. Previously he could remain submerged only for as long as he could hold his breath. Nowadays most of those who venture beneath the seas wear some form of protective clothing, usually a rubber suit, and so they no longer dive 'in the skin'. Nonetheless the word 'skindiving' has been retained and this has caused a little confusion because it now means different things to different people. To some it means diving with fins, mask and snorkel, and in this book we shall refer to diving with this simple basic equipment as *snorkelling*. To others, 'skindiving' means diving with an aqualung, and in this book the word *skindiving* will be used in its most widely understood context which is swimming underwater with an aqualung for sport and pleasure.

Left *skindiving off Sark in the Channel Islands*

Inner space

Man has an instinct to explore — to discover new frontiers. Man has been tramping around the surface of the earth for about one million years and during that time he has infiltrated even the remotest regions. For centuries he has sailed on the lakes and on the seas, exploring coastlines and distant islands. Often the coastlines he explored were hot, barren and inhospitable; such areas as the Red Sea and the Persian Gulf. The water provided a highway along which men could travel. He did not know that beneath him, there was often a cool wonderland full of light, life and dazzling colour; but that world, just a few feet under the surface of the sea, was as remote and inaccessible as outer space; and like outer space, the inner space of the undersea world had to wait for the twentieth century before Man invaded it. Until relatively recently men knew of the existence of the undersea world, but had no means of getting there.

For me, the infinite variety of shapes and different forms of life that make up the world of the sea are far more interesting than the lifeless vacuum of outer space. It costs millions of pounds and an enormous amount of fuel to put a single man on the moon. The exciting world of inner space can be discovered by anyone who visits the sea.

It was the development of the rocket that enabled men to leave our planet and explore the space beyond. The key to the door of inner space was remarkably simple — as simple and fundamental as the wheel — it was a pair of goggles.

Goggling

Those readers who have swum underwater with their eyes open will know that, although it is possible to make out objects below the surface, they can only be seen as blurred shapes. This is because our eyes have evolved to see in air, not in water. The first non-professional diver to discover the importance of seeing clearly in the sea was Guy Gilpatric, an American. He made his discovery in the South of France in the nineteen thirties. He put on a pair of watertight flying goggles, sank feet first into the sea and found that the underwater world was revealed with unexpected clarity. It was as if he was looking through the glass wall of an enormous aquarium; he had discovered the beautiful world of inner space and had developed a very simple way of getting there. As he was a writer and journalist he promptly set about telling the world of his discovery and the adventures that he was having.

The secret of his discovery lay in the fact that a pair of goggles excluded the water so that his eyes were always in contact with air, and were therefore able to funcion as they did on land. Guy Gilpatric called his new-found sport 'goggling' — for obvious reasons. He coupled his underwater explorations with the adventure of hunting with a spear; and goggle fishing, as it was called, became popular, I might say, too popular. Many people took to the water with spears, and later with powerful spearguns. In some areas, the populations of certain species of fish, that lived in restricted territories on the seabed, were decimated. The underwater fishermen were like the first explorers, armed with guns, in Africa and in the New World. They shot at anything and everything. They believed that wildlife was inexhaustible and that nature would rapidly replenish the stocks. As we now know, this is not the case. When too many people start killing wildlife, on the land or in the sea, the very thing that attracts people to wild places, i.e. the wild animals and plants, disappears. Although people still hunt to kill, more and more hunters are shooting with a camera — not a gun — both above and below water. In many countries, seabed nature reserves are being established, so that people can again enjoy seeing the same rich variety of life that the pioneers found a few decades ago.

Below *in the underwater world, the diver is weightless.*

Opposite page *an underwater garden in the Mediterranean.*

Snorkelling

The early sport of goggling has now evolved into what we call snorkel swimming. For the investment of just a few pounds in equipment, any person can enjoy healthy exercise and at the same time become an explorer of the underwater world. You do not have to be a superman to enjoy underwater swimming. Indeed, many swimmers have found it easier to learn to swim using the basic equipment of mask, fins and snorkel, than to learn with no swimming aids.

Equipment for snorkelling

As with all sports, in the long run it pays to buy good equipment and it is preferable to purchase it from a specialist shop. There are now diving shops in most big towns, and many of them carry a large selection of basic diving equipment. The shop assistant will be able to give you sound advice and help you to make the best choice. However, before you make your purchase it is as well to know the function of the items you require. So let's look at each in turn.

First and most important is the *facemask*.

Guy Gilpatric used goggles for his diving escapades. Goggles are still available but are far inferior to a facemask which encloses the nose. As the diver descends, the water above him increases the pressure on his body. This squashes the mask on to his face unless the pressure is equalised by gently exhaling through the nose. It is impossible to do this with goggles. They are therefore less comfortable to wear and can be dangerous if used at depths.

No two people have the same shapes to their faces, so the selection of a facemask is important if it is to be a comfortable and watertight fit. The rubber flange on many facemasks has a feather edge enabling it to fit most faces; others have a double edge to give an even better seal. You may be offered a dozen models of mask to choose from in a diving shop. It is well worth trying on several masks to find one which is really comfortable to wear. In addition to being comfortable a facemask must, of course, be leakproof. An easy way to test this is to fit the mask to the face without the strap in position, and gently inhale through the nose. If the mask is a good

The diver may be confronted with a wide choice of masks of varying price.

8

The first stage in snorkelling: float on the surface of the water with your hands by your sides and move forward with a gentle crawl stroke of the fins.

watertight fit it will stay sealed to the face without support. When you breathe out through your nose the inside and outside pressures will equalise, and the mask will have to be held in position.

Some masks are fitted with plastic, usually perspex, windows. The advantage of these is that they are unlikely to shatter, they do, however, have a nasty habit of misting up. This can be prevented by periodically applying demisting fluid, but it is far better to eliminate the fault altogether, and choose a mask with a safety-glass window.

People with poor eyesight can have lenses stuck to the face plate. It is also possible to buy special spectacle frames which can be attached to the inside of the mask. Those who are only slightly short-sighted will find there is no need to correct their vision as underwater objects appear bigger and closer, and the total visible distance underwater seldom exceeds 30 metres anyway.

Some masks are fitted with separate side windows to give maximum peripheral vision, but my personal experience is that such masks, which are often the most expensive, offer no significant benefits. The field of vision can, however, be increased by placing the faceplate closer to the eyes. This has been achieved in some masks by shaping the faceplate like a flat inverted U. The modified rubber flange is shaped to enclose the nose which extends beyond the faceplate. Most masks are designed in such a manner that the nose can be pinched to clear the ears. This feature is important if the snorkeller intends to take up aqualung diving.

The latest trend in mask design is to reduce the volume of air inside the mask to a minimum. By reducing this 'dead space', as it is called, less air has to pass into the mask from the lungs to equalise the external pressure. This is only important for more advanced snorkel divers, who may go to depths where the external pressure considerably reduces the volume of air inside the lungs. The beginner spends most of his time floating on the surface 'looking in'; he should find plenty to interest him in the shallows and will have no need to descend below 6 metres.

The mask enables you to see clearly underwater. When lying face down on the surface your nose is inside the mask and your mouth is submerged. In this position you cannot inhale without lifting your head clear of the water. The *snorkel* enables you to get air in and out of your lungs without the irksome need to repeatedly lift your head clear of the water. The snorkel tube extends the opening of your mouth to the back of your head. In humans this device is an optional extra; in whales and dolphins it is permanently built in as part of their anatomy.

The snorkel is a simple open tube, usually made of plastic, with a rubber mouthpiece. The mouthpiece consists of two rubber spigots which are gripped between the teeth, and a rubber flange which is held between the gums and lips, forming a watertight seal.

Do not buy a snorkel tube with fancy valves on it. They are quite unnecessary and likely to go wrong. Ping-pong balls in rubber cages are definitely not recommended, nor are masks with built-in snorkels. A snorkel tube with a walking stick shape is simple and efficient. When it comes to buying diving equipment I am an advocate of the old adage 'the simpler the better' — with the proviso, of course, that the equipment is well-made, comfortable and fulfils its function.

Fins provide the snorkel swimmer with his propulsive power and at the same time give him considerable manoeuvrability. One has only to look at a film of a seal swimming to see how effective fins are. A good pair of rubber fins will convert the poorest swimmer into a champion. They make the most efficient use of the leg muscles for propelling the diver through the water.

Fins should be made of good quality rubber and not too floppy. Most divers prefer fins with a shoe fitting to those with heel straps. If you intend to buy a full rubber suit remember that your fins will have to fit over your bootees. Fins with tight fitting shoes not only become uncomfortable after a period of swimming, they become agonising. So it is better to choose a pair that is too slack in the shoe than too tight. You can always wear a pair of socks if your fins are uncomfortably loose.

Learning to snorkel
Well that's your basic snorkelling equipment sorted out. Now how do you go about learning to use it?

That depends on how old you are and where you live.

I would strongly recommend that when you first try out snorkel swimming, you either do so with a friend who has already mastered the techniques, or get instruction at a diving school. Better still you could join a diving club where underwater swimming

Your passport to adventure is a set of basic equipment: fins, mask and snorkel.

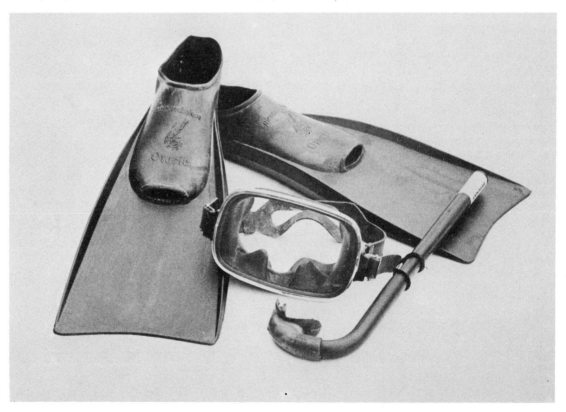

is a common interest. The British Sub-Aqua Club (BSAC) has branches in many parts of the world, in addition to those throughout Great Britain, and its standards of training are of the highest order.

Young people can join the National Snorkellers Club (NSC) which has branches throughout the country. Many of the branches are in schools where children are taught by school teachers who have qualified as NSC instructors.

Upon joining the National Snorkellers Club, members are recommended to buy a copy of the British Sub-Aqua Club Snorkelling Manual, which covers such subjects as rescue and resuscitation. The pupil must be familiar with these subjects, and prove that he is competent in the water, before he can qualify for his National Snorkellers' Certificate.

Although many people find it easier to learn to swim with mask, fins and snorkel, the National Snorkellers Club expect a high standard of swimming proficiency before members begin serious snorkel training. The British Sub-Aqua Club 'A' test is generally considered to be the minimum requirement. It should be practised until it can be performed in a single pool session. Here is what you will be expected to do:

(1) Swim 200 metres using any front stroke.
(2) Swim 100 metres using any back stroke.
(3) Swim 50 metres wearing a weight belt (maximum 5 kilos, adjusted according to build).
(4) Tread water for one minute with hands above the head.
(6) Dive six times to the bottom of the pool to retrieve an object (2 metres is a resonable depth).

This test may appear severe. It is, and for a good reason: if you loose part of your equipment, perhaps a fin when you are snorkelling in the sea, your instructor must be sure that you are capable of swimming safely back to the shore.

I was a keen swimmer before I took up snorkelling, so I had no problems passing the 'A' test when I first joined the British Sub-Aqua Club. For me the most difficult part of snorkel training was learning to breathe through my mouth. However, after a few trial sessions with my head submerged in the sink in the bathroom at home I soon mastered it; and I have never looked back since.

New masks tend to mist-up. So I recommend that you wash your new mask in soapy water and then thoroughly rinse it before you wear it. The standard procedure to prevent misting thereafter is to spit into

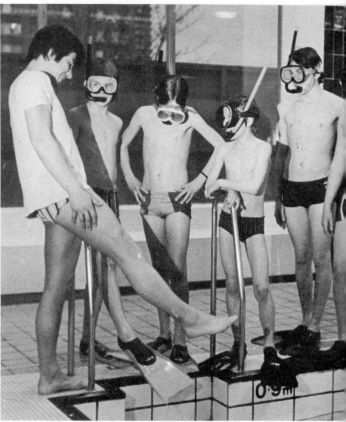

Above right *Lionel Blandford, founder of the National Snorkellers Club, instructs a group of members at a London swimming pool.* Right *young snorkellers receive their first instruction: the legs should be kept almost straight and a crawl stroke used when snorkelling.*

The function of the mask is carefully explained to a group of snorkellers on a diving holiday in Kenya.

the mask and spread a thin film of saliva over the inner surface of the glass. The mask is then dipped into the water before it is positioned on your face. Any hair that finds its way under the rubber flange should be pulled free to ensure a good seal with the face.

If your snorkel tube does not have a rubber retainer with which to attach it to the mask, push the snorkel tube under the headstrap. Put the mouthpiece in position and adjust the snorkel tube so that it is comfortable to wear. Some snorkel tubes are deflected slightly above the U bend and are intended for use on only one side of the face, so if you have one of these make sure it is the right way round. When it is correctly placed, the open end of the tube will be upright when you are floating on the surface of the water with your head looking slightly forward.

With your facemask in position practise breathing through your snorkel tube before fitting your fins and launching yourself into the water.

When you are in the water, lie on the surface looking down. Propel yourself through the water with up and down strokes of your fins. Keep your legs almost straight, flexing your knees only slightly. After a while you will feel the correct stroke because

it will give maximum forward propulsion with the minimum of effort. Do not try to push yourself through the water as if you were pedalling a bicycle.

To dive from the surface, breathe in, dip your head and shoulders sharply downwards with your hands straight ahead. At the same time raise your legs out of the water and allow their weight in air to push you smoothly down. As soon as your feet are submerged start finning.

Stop descending if your ears hurt. To clear them, blow gently through your nose. As soon as you surface, blow out sharply through your mouth. This will clear any water in your snorkel tube and you can then inhale in comfort.

When you feel comfortable and confident when wearing the equipment in the water try different methods of entry from the side of the pool. The simplest is to step boldly forward over the water, holding your mask to prevent it being swept off as it hits the surface. Alternative methods are to sit on the side of the pool and gently roll, forwards or backwards, into the water.

Some people pick up snorkelling within ten minutes; others need two or three sessions before they master the basics. Most people gain confidence remarkably quickly, especially under the guidance of a good instructor.

If you happen to be at the seaside at this stage in your training then it is time to make your first foray into the sea; but remember that over confidence at this early stage can be dangerous. Be aware of your inexperience and stay in the shallows. An unexpected lung full of water could cause a brief coughing spasm which is very unpleasant. You will be thankful that you can stand on the bottom until it clears.

When you can take such a situation in your stride, whether you are in a pool or in the sea, it is time to start improving your snorkelling technique. Fish are wild animals and they have a strong instinct for survival. Like animals on land they take flight if you are noisy or clumsy. Sounds do travel underwater, so first practice swimming with the minimum of disturbance on the surface. Keep your fins just submerged and don't splash. Practise your duck dive from the surface until you can slide into the water as silently as an arrow. Finally, make sure that you can clear a flooded mask easily and quickly, even when you are submerged. To do this, position yourself vertically in the water and tilt your head slightly backwards. In this position any water in the mask will flow to the bottom. Next, hold your mask gently against your forehead and exhale slowly through your nose. The air passing

These three pictures were taken by Horace Dobbs for the British Sub-Aqua Club Snorkelling Manual. They illustrate different methods of entry into the water. People who take up snorkelling are recommended to join the BSAC National Snorkellers Club.

into the mask will then displace the water downwards and the mask will clear in a second or two.

Safety in the water

With practice you will find that the time you can remain underwater gradually increases. Your diving time will vary depending on how tired, or how cold you are. When you are tired and cold your body burns up food and oxygen at a faster rate, so the time you can stay submerged becomes shorter. You should never stay underwater for so long that you are absolutely bursting to come up. To do so could be very dangerous.

The compulsion to breathe in is stimulated by the level of carbon dioxide in the blood. The respiratory centre in the brain responds to high carbon dioxide levels and commands your lungs to breathe in. It is a very sensitive mechanism and if you do not allow your lungs to obey, you could black out. If, on the other hand, you cannot resist the desire to breathe and you inhale water, you could drown.

Trained athletes sometimes breathe deeply in and out for several minutes before subjecting themselves to a short period of very strenuous exercise. This procedure is called *hyperventilation*. It flushes the carbon dioxide from the blood and reduces the rate of breathing during the subsequent short bursts of

Young snorkellers are · given instruction in a London swimming pool.

exercise. If, however, the athlete's body becomes too short of oxygen (a condition known as hypoxia) an in-built safety mechanism comes into operation: the athlete blacks out. This immediately stops the cause of the excessive demand for oxygen and he will remain unconscious until his bodily functions are within their normal capacity again. For an athlete a blackout is nature's warning that he has gone too far, and if he has any sense he will heed the warning. The underwater swimmer who blacks out is seldom given the opportunity to heed such a warning, if it happens when he is underwater he is dead within minutes.

The moral is simple: *don't hyperventilate before snorkel diving.*

Now, although you may be sensible and not hyperventilate, you cannot be sure that everyone else will abide by this rule. Also there are unexpected circumstances, such as a fit or a heart attack, which may cause a snorkeller to become unconscious in the water. When this happens a speedy rescue is of the utmost importance. Brain cells rapidly die if they are starved of oxygen, so literally every second counts: you must get the victim breathing again as soon as possible.

The method that is now universally accepted as the most effective way of restoring breathing in a drowning person is known by its initials E.A.R. — which stand for *Expired Air Resuscitation*. It involves blowing directly into the drowning person's lungs. To do this, the rescuer can either

All divers should learn the techniques of livesaving and resuscitation.

pinch the subject's nose with his fingers and blow into the lungs via the mouth, or the rescuer may put his mouth over the subject's nose and blow into the lungs whilst sealing the subject's mouth with a cheek.

To fully understand the principles of EAR, you should practise the methods on land under the supervision of a qualified instructor.

If you are faced with a real life emergency and you need to give artificial respiration, watch to see that the air you are blowing into your subject is not going into his stomach instead of his lungs. If this happens you will notice a swelling at the base of the ribs. To expel the air, gently push on the swelling and continue giving one breath every five seconds.

It is of the utmost importance to get air to the lungs as soon as possible; so if you are rescuing an unconscious person in the water your first action, once you have raised him to the surface, should be to commence EAR immediately — in the water. Give four short breaths in quick succession, pause and then give one breath about once every five seconds. When you have got into a rhythm you can start to tow the subject ashore, keeping his mouth and nose above water at all times. Hopefully, by this time you will have somebody alongside you who can help with the tow and with getting the victim ashore.

Knowing how to save a person from drowning should be learned and practised by all snorkel swimmers and aqualung divers. One day you may be the one who is brought back from the brink of death.

The most common cause of drowning is panic. A person on the brink of panic will usually tread water furiously. He may take unwanted gulps of water. When this happens he may shout or wave his arms frantically in the air. Unfortunately the weight of his arms in the air will cause him to sink and to take even more choking gulps of water.

When attempting to rescue such a person it is obviously essential to reach them with the utmost speed. Using an overarm crawl in addition to fins is probably the best way. When you arrive it is important that you should be in fit state to perform a rescue, so make sure that you yourself are composed. If he is in a state of severe panic the subject could be violent, so avoid contact with him from the front. Approach cautiously from the rear and grasp him firmly from behind keeping his head above the water. He may be struggling frantically, but he will soon regain his confidence when he realises that he is in capable hands. When he has quietened he is ready for towing ashore.

The British Sub-Aqua Club has a slogan which states *YOU ARE SAFER WITH A DIVER ON THE BEACH.* The sound sense behind this slogan can be appreciated when one considers how much more efficiently a swimmer will perform a rescue when he is wearing a pair of fins. Rescue techniques and methods of artificial respiration are all part of the diver's training programme.

More advanced snorkel training
The British Sub-Aqua Club 'B' test is designed to test ability to use basic equipment effectively. It also shows whether a snorkeller is able to cope with different emergency situations. Even if you are not a member of the BSAC it is worth trying their tests to see if you measure up to their standards. This is what you have to do:

1. Sink all equipment in the deep end of the pool, dive for each item in turn and fit at the surface, without support.
2. Fin 200 metres, surface diving every 25 metres.
3. Tow a subject as big as yourself 50 metres by a BSAC method, which incorporates expired air resuscitation in the water, giving at least two or three effective breaths over this distance.
4. Land the subject and continue EAR on the side of the pool.
5. Perform three forward and three backward rolls in the water.
6. Fin 15 metres under water.
7. Hold your breath for 30 seconds under water.

If you can carry out the 'B' test without too much difficulty you should have no problems when you progress to the next stage — the 'C' test. If you are fit, and a reasonably strong swimmer, the only section of the 'C' test that is likely to cause trouble is section 3 which entails swimming with face submerged, using a snorkel tube, but no facemask. It is one of those techniques that comes, like learning to ride a bicycle. Sometimes it takes a little perseverence to acquire the knack, but once you've mastered it you can always do it. It is something you should be able to do in case your mask should accidentally become flooded. Mastery of breathing without difficulty through the mouth when the face is submerged is an essential preliminary to aqualung training.

Each one of the exercises in the 'C' test must be carried out in succession, without resting or taking support. Here they are:

1. Fin 50 metres wearing a weight belt (maximum 5 kilos but this can be adjusted according to build).
2. Release the weight belt in the deep end and

Anyone who goes on holiday to the seaside, where the water is clear, will miss a wonderful experience if they do not 'look in' to the underwater world. Stephanie Ponsford, a travel writer, prepares to go snorkelling during a job assignment to Mauritius.

Hold the mask on to your face when you jump in from a height, otherwise the mask may become dislodged when you hit the water.

remove your mask.
3. Fin 50 metres with your face submerged, using a snorkel tube but no mask.
4. Complete at the deep end, replace your mask, surface dive, recover and refit the weight belt.
5. Give the signal 'I am OK'.
6. Fin a further 50 metres wearing the same weightbelt as used before.

Octopush

Although completion of the three snorkel tests is a good end point in training, it is only the beginning of the fun you can have once you have become a proficient snorkeller. For most snorkellers the highlight of their year is the annual summer holiday at the seaside. But what do trained snorkellers do to keep fit between the summer visits to the coast?

In 1954 a group of divers in Southsea decided that, during the winter months, they wanted to do something more exciting than swim up and down in a swimming pool, so they invented a game; and they called it OCTOPUSH.

Octopush is played by two teams of six snorkellers. The nearest game to it on land is ice hockey. Instead of a puck the players use a lead disc called a squid. The squid is pushed and flicked along the floor of the pool with a small bat called a pusher. The objective of the game is to get the squid into the opponents' goal, which is not called a goal but a gulley. Scored goals are called gulls.

The rules of the game are simple and a rulebook can be obtained from British Sub-Aqua Club Headquarters. The rules state that the squid should never be handled by a player and that it should always stay on the bottom of the pool during play. The game can become very boisterous and there are penalties if a player grips or attempts to remove another player's equipment. A foul is committed if a player deliberately strikes or impedes another player. No player is allowed to stand in shallow water for a rest while the game is in play. A match lasts for 22 minutes, consisting of 10 minutes each way with a 2 minute half-time break. The game is supervised by a snorkelling referee who is assisted by two marshals. They remain in the pool during play. A player who commits a foul may be sent out of the water for 2 minutes during play. In extreme cases he may be ordered out of the water for the rest of the match.

Octopush is a fast game, and as in all such sports, tactics are as important as sheer physical stamina. During each winter season, diving clubs from different parts of the country battle with one another in the Octopush League.

Eleven year old Emma Holtby snorkels in the Indian Ocean.

John Cadd made an excellent film entitled 'Octopush' for his diploma when studying at the Harrow College of Technology and Art. His film certainly captures the pace and excitement of the game. The film is now available from the BSAC 16mm Film Library.

If you can survive a hard fought game of octopush you have achieved a high degree of snorkelling proficiency that will hold you in good stead for the next steps along the upside-down ladder of progress in skindiving — snorkelling in the sea and aqualung diving.

No protection against the cold is necessary when you snorkel in tropical seas.

Snorkelling in the Sea

I mastered snorkelling and the techniques of aqualung diving during the winter months of 1957. The following year I waited, with increasing expectancy, for our family holiday to South Devon. I owned only the basic equipment of fins, mask and snorkel, and an underwater housing I had made for my camera.

I still recall the pure magic of my early snorkel dives in the sea. Hope Cove was one of my favourite spots. Within easy reach of the shore were underwater gardens of waving seaweed. Long filaments of dark green thongweed and the swaying broad leaves of deep red seaweeds mixed with the delicate, pale, translucent green of the sea lettuce in a symphony of colour and movement. This vegetation grew in profusion on a rockery, set in clean yellow sand. Beautiful rainbow coloured fish, which I later found out were wrasse, nibbled at unseen particles on the rocks. Sometimes they took no notice of me. At other times they would dart away as I approached. As I swam forward my constantly changing horizon vanished into a zircon-blue sea.

I wore no protective clothing. When I first entered the sea I would feel the familiar cold grip of the water. Then the sensation of cold passed, and I forgot all about it as I wandered alone through my own enchanted underwater garden. I snorkelled down into the gulleys, looking for spider crabs that lurked in crannies in the rocks. There was always something new to see.

The pure magic lasted for about 15 minutes. During that time my mind seemed to be detached from my body. I was unaware that I was rapidly losing heat. Then the first feeling of discomfort would intrude. After about 20 minutes from first stepping into the sea I began to feel distinctly chilled, and after half an hour could withstand the cold no longer. I was forced to return to the beach to warm

Denis Moor snorkels down 9 metres off the coast of Sardinia. With a little practice, most snorkel divers can reach this depth, many can go much deeper.

19

Opposite page *snorkel divers can explore coral gardens such as this one which is off the coast of Florida.*

Below *a fully equipped snorkel diver*

through — which sometimes took an hour, or even longer.

For two summers I enjoyed the pleasure and suffered the cold. During the following winter months, however, I made myself a wetsuit of quarter inch thick sponge neoprene. I tried it out on the first day of our next holiday. Once I was in the sea, time lost all meaning. After what seemed to be about half an hour, I made my way back to the beach. When I arrived, there were scenes of great activity and excitement. A boat was being brought down to the water's edge. My wife was having a serious debate with the owner, and pointing to the long line of rocks that edged the bay. When she saw me she was relieved and angry. 'Where on earth have you been?' she said, 'You have been gone for over two hours and I have just started to organise a search party'.

Be seen
Like many of the pioneer skindivers, I learned by experience, and I have modified my diving practice accordingly. My wetsuit, and all the other equipment that I wore were black, so it was very difficult for a person on the shore to spot me. The yellow rubber tape, now often used to reinforce the seams of diving suits, makes the diver stand out better against the background. It also avoids the sort of accident that happened to a fellow diver, who nearly lost his life when a man with a gun on the shore thought that the black head he saw bobbing about in the sea belonged to a seal. He opened fire. Fortunately another diver was on hand to rescue the wounded man.

When you are diving in the sea, it is sensible to wear a loose fluorescent red hood over your rubber hood.

Wear a watch
A watch will, of course, enable you to keep track of the time you spend in the water. When buying a watch, be sure that it is a proper diving watch and not just waterproof. Some watches, which look like proper diving watches, are designed only to keep out the water if they are splashed in a washbasin. A diving watch must be both waterproof and pressure resistant. The most common area of leakage is round the winder, so the best diving watches have a screw-down winder and are fitted with a rotating bezel. The bezel is a disc fitted around the rim of the face of the watch. It is simply a memory aid. It can be set either to indicate the position of the minute hand when you enter the water, or to indicate the time you intend to leave the water.

Tow a buoy
Towing a buoy is a safety precaution that I stongly advocate for the snorkeller in the sea, particularly if he goes off on his own. You can buy inflatable buoys

made from brightly coloured plastic. An old car inner tube, or a child's swimming ring, is a satisfactory makeshift alternative especially if a flag is attached. This safety aid can have several functions. A plastic net shopping bag underneath it becomes a useful container for such objects as a spare weight, or a camera.

A towed buoy can become a lifesaver. If you happen to get caught in a sudden tidal run and swept away from the shore, you can hang on to the buoy until you are rescued, or swim ashore again. The greatest value of a buoy may be to protect you from a relatively new hazard — the speedboat. This is much more of a threat in the Mediterranean than it is around British shores. Nonetheless, wherever you snorkel dive, be alert to the danger. Speedboats travel so fast that they can appear to come from nowhere in seconds. If the boat is towing a water skier the man at the wheel may be concentrating more on what is going on behind him than what is in his path. Most speedboat drivers are sensible and thoroughly aware of their responsibilities to others. However, if it is your misfortune to be in the path of one of the rare unthinking, unobservant maniacs, it may be your last dive. In this situation a brightly coloured buoy is the best insurance of survival.

Keep warm

Cold is a discomfort that can be endured for a certain period of time, but it should not be endured for too long. If your teeth start to chatter, and you begin to shiver, it is time to leave the water. These are Nature's warning signals and they occur when your body temperature starts to drop. To conserve heat, the supply of warm blood to the extremities is automatically reduced, and when this happens the strength of the arms and legs diminishes. The cold diver becomes progressively weaker. He is often quite unaware of this until he has to make an extra effort, or needs to carry out a task that requires manual dexterity. Then he could get into difficulties, if, for instance, he needed to use his knife and could not pull it out of its sheath.

A diving suit is the answer to heat loss problems. Most snorkel divers wear what is known as a wetsuit. Wetsuits are made of sponge neoprene, although they were first used by skindivers, the advantages of wetsuits have been recognised by participants in other sports. Almost identical suits are now worn by water skiers, yachtsmen, cave explorers, in fact all sportsmen who are likely to get both cold and wet.

Wetsuits

Wetsuits are not so called because they get wet on the outside. Their name derives from the fact that

Below young Melanie Dobbs heads for the surface. When she surfaces she must clear any water from her snorkel tube before she inhales.

Opposite page a family of snorkellers look down into the inner space of the Indian Ocean.

they can also become wet on the inside. In the early days of amateur diving divers attempted to keep warm with suits of rubberised fabric that were designed to completely exclude the water i.e. drysuits. Warm clothes were worn underneath and the water was excluded with soft rubber seals that were a close fit around the neck and wrists. There were a number of disadvantages to those early dry suits. They were very uncomfortable to wear at depth. Also, if they were badly punctured they quickly became very inefficient wetsuits.

When the wetsuit was introduced the need to keep the body of the diver absolutely dry was no longer of paramount importance. The diver was insulated, not by the air trapped between the suit and his body, but by the thousands of tiny bubbles of air within the rubber sponge of the wetsuit. The thicker the sponge the more effective was the insulation, so when a diver put on a wetsuit the small amount of water that trickled in was of little consequence.

Most of the early wetsuits were made to measure. Nowadays the need for a good fit is sometimes overlooked and I have seen divers wearing baggy suits with gaping holes in them. Water will pump in and out of suits with tears or ill-fitting jackets and trousers. When this happens the diver soon looses the valuable heat he is trying to conserve.

Most good diving shops will offer you a range of wetsuits. For those who restrict themselves to short spells in the sea, or confine their diving activities to the Mediterranean, a relatively thin jacket is all that is required. If, however, you intend to use the suit in British waters and wish to progress to aqualung diving, you should have a complete diving suit including long johns, hood and bootees.

· For those with a limited budget, some shops sell kits from which the diver can make his own wetsuit. Suppliers of DIY materials can also be found in the diving journals (*Triton* and *Sub-Aqua Magazine* in the UK). Making a wetsuit is not difficult. Sheets of neoprene can be easily cut with a pair of scissors. Joins are made by applying a special adhesive (Evostick is a good substitute) to the cut edges. When the glue has become very tacky the edges are butted together. Joins can be strengthened by stitching or by covering with tape.

Neoprene does not slide easily over human skin. Early wetsuits had to be lubricated, usually with talc, before they were put on. Nowadays, most wetsuits have a nylon fabric lining which makes getting kitted-up much easier. Some suits have nylon skins

Left a wetsuit must be worn by snorkellers who dive for long periods in the cold seas around the British coast. A young member of the National Snorkellers Club demonstrates the full equipment.

on both surfaces, enabling them to be worn with either side outermost.

Weightbelts

Imagine a wetsuit screwed up into a ball about the size of a large football. Then imagine what would happen if you tossed it into the sea and tried to push it under the surface. You would need considerable force to hold it under the water and as soon as you let go, it would spring back to the surface. Now put yourself inside the suit. What happens when you try to swim down? You bob up like a cork. The same force is required to keep you down as is required to keep the rolled-up suit submerged.

This situation may be good from a safety point of view but it certainly isn't good if you want to snorkel down and explore. To do that, with the minimum of effort, you need to be what is called 'neutrally buoyant'. That is, you neither sink, nor float, but, when you are not swimming, remain suspended in the water. To counteract the buoyancy of your suit you must wear a weightbelt.

A weightbelt consists of a number of lead weights threaded, or screwed on to a belt, which is fitted with a quick-release fastening. A weightbelt should be regarded as an expendable item that can be jettisoned in an emergency. Once the weightbelt has been discarded a diver wearing a wetsuit will float easily on the surface.

A knife

What other equipment should a snorkel diver take with him in the sea? A knife is generally regarded as essential.

Most divers favour a sheath knife that is strapped to the leg. I prefer a knife which is retained with a strong rubber loop round the handle as it is less likely to be lost than one which is held in the sheath with a clip.

Diving knives come in a variety of shapes and weights. Most of them are made of stainless, or stain resistant steel. I have found that I use my diving knife most frequently when I am out of the water for jobs ranging from buttering pieces of bread to opening cans when I have forgotten a tin opener. I quite often use it for cutting heavy ropes and prefer a knife which has one serrated, or saw edge, which is better for this purpose.

I regard my knife as an essential piece of my diving equipment and I feel slightly uneasy if ever I go into the water without it. The nylon line used by anglers is almost invisible in water. It is easy to swim into it and get snagged. Although, when this has happened I have always managed to break free easily, I was always reassured by the knowledge that I could escape with a deft stroke of my knife.

Most divers regard a knife as an essential part of their equipment.

A weightbelt, such as this one, must have a quick-release fastening.

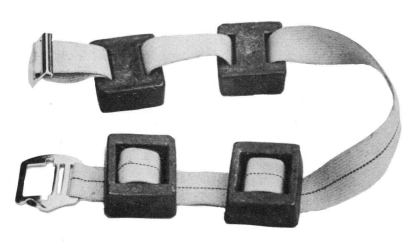

Thirteen year old Ashley Dobbs plays with a wild dolphin while snorkelling off the British coast

Two snorkel divers explore the shallow waters of a coral lagoon.

A lifejacket

To wear a lifejacket and a wetsuit may appear at first glance to be taking safety too far, but those who organise snorkelling holidays and expeditions generally make it a rule that everyone must wear a lifejacket.

When a good lifejacket is inflated it tips the diver's head slightly backwards, so that if a diver becomes unconscious for any reason, he floats on his back with his nose and mouth clear of the water. Also, a tired diver may feel the need for a little buoyancy when he is swimming back to base.

Weightbelts are not cheap and, unless the situation becomes serious, most snorkellers would rather inflate their lifejacket than jettison their weights. A lifejacket with a mouth inflation tube is useful because sufficient air can be blown into it to keep the snorkeller comfortably afloat.

Common sense

For the snorkel diver who must have everything there are numerous other items he can attach to himself. They include such things as a compass, a torch, a notepad, a thermometer, a depth gauge, a camera, an exposure meter and even a metal hook. He may go into the water decked out like a Christmas tree. Yet there is one item which is more important than all others and which is not on that list. I have not mentioned it so far and it costs nothing: it is simple common sense.

The sea is there for everyone to enjoy. Anglers have as much right to cast their lines into the sea as you have to dive in it. Don't cause friction and conflict by swimming too close to their lines. It is far better to make a friend than an enemy, so if you get the opportunity talk to the fishermen. Viewed from their own perspective, they often have a wealth of knowledge on fish and other forms of life in the sea, and they are usually very willing to listen to somebody who can tell them what the underwater world is like from the inside.

Boats on the move are always dangerous. So stay away from them. This is very important in harbours. Never swim across the entrance to a harbour. Boat traffic can go in either direction at any time. Steering a boat is not like driving a car. Much more skill and judgement are required to bring a boat safely up to a mooring. A wrong move could cause it to hole on some submerged rocks. Most boatmen take great pride in their skill, and when they come into harbour they know that many friendly but critical eyes are upon them. Their aim is to bring the boat up to the jetty with barely a bump, so coming into harbour is a dangerous moment of high tension. A snorkeller in their path can expect a broadside of invective. Your common sense should tell you to keep well clear.

Harbour Masters are a law unto themselves and they can be intolerant of amateur divers. A Harbour Master is responsible for the smooth safe running of his harbour. The British Sub-Aqua Club have gone to considerable lengths to improve relations between divers and Harbour Masters. They have been successful, but, as we all know, it takes a lot of time to build up a really good relationship, and that relationship can be strained by a single thoughtless act. If you wish to dive in a harbour consult the Harbour Master first. If he says no, then accept his decision gracefully. There is always a chance that he may ask you to help him, by, for example, freeing a rope that has fouled a propellor. In my own dealings with Harbour Masters, I have found them to be, without exception, both reasonable and very helpful, but like all people in authority they like to be kept informed.

I hope that your common sense will tell you to be on the look out for currents in tidal areas. Tidal currents vary with phase of the moon, the time of the day and the topography of coastal areas. Tidal flow is usually non-existant, or at a minimum at high water and low water. The times of high and low water, which vary from one place to another, can be obtained from the nearest Harbour Master. Alternatively, a booklet of tide tables can be purchased locally; shops that sell fishing tackle usually have them in stock.

Tidal flow is seldom a problem to snorkellers who confine their activities to sheltered bays. The danger lies round headlands that project well into the sea. In such areas a tidal flow can set in very quickly, so always be on the alert. It is deceptively easy to swim with the tide and very tiring to swim against it. Be on the look out for signs of strong tidal flow, such as the seaweeds continuously streaming in one direction. If you do find yourself caught in a tidal run remember that the flow is usually less very close inshore, so hug the rocks on your return route until you reach still water.

The more frequently you snorkel in the sea the greater will be the respect you have for it. The sea is a wonderful playground in which you can enjoy hours of snorkelling pleasure. If common sense and constant alertness are the companions you always take with you, you will come back safely.

A young snorkel diver finds a piece of coral while diving off the coast of Kenya

Aqualung Diving

The aqualung

As soon as the first goggle divers discovered the joys and beauty of the underwater world they started to look for a way to stay submerged for longer periods. They looked at the old 'hard hat' sponge divers who could stay down for long periods; but the traditional divers were not free divers: they tramped across the seabed in heavy lead-soled boots and restricting rubberised canvas suits, and their heads were encapsulated in copper helmets. For their survival they relied entirely upon a surface crew and upon a supply of air pumped into their helmets via rubber hoses connected to compressors. With all this paraphernalia they were as restricted as the first astronaut space walkers who were tied to their spaceships by their umbilicals.

Opposite page *aqualung diving in the clear waters of the Red Sea.*

Below left *this steel aqualung cylinder has an integral carrying handle and reserve.* Centre *an aluminium alloy cylinder with reserve: a reserve is essential if the Continental European practice is followed of diving without a pressure gauge on the regulator. When breathing becomes difficult the diver pulls the reserve lever which is attached to the neck of the cylinder. This opens the reserve and allows the diver enough air to make an unhurried ascent.* Right *a Twinset: this is comfortable to wear, but no reserve is fitted so a diver must use a demand valve with a pressure gauge.*

A group of divers set off to explore a coral reef. Each diver is using a single hose regulator. The diver on the right wears an ABLJ, a diving watch and a depth gauge.

Right *a single hose regulator with a mouth piece retaining strap* Below *a twin hose demand valve with a mouth piece retaining strap*

The new explorers of the inner space of the sea wanted the best of both worlds: the freedom of the sporting goggle fisherman and the underwater duration of the professional Greek sponge divers.

The problem to be resolved was a technical one. The deeper a diver descends, the greater is the pressure on his body. As a man can only breathe in and out against a small pressure difference he needs a self-contained supply that delivers air to him at exactly the same pressure as his surroundings — regardless of the depth.

The source of air was no problem. It was easy to compress air into a cylinder to a pressure far in excess of the requirements imposed by the depths. The difficulty was to bleed the air from the cylinder gently into the divers lungs.

The breakthrough came with the development of a valve that contained a rubber diaphragm which was open to the atmosphere in air, and to the water in the sea. When the external pressure increased the diaphragm, being rubber, deflected. This movement actuated a series of tiny levers that allowed air to escape from the high pressure cylinder into a small chamber behind the diaphragm. When the inside and outside pressures were again equal the diaphragm moved back into a neutral position which automatically stopped the flow of air into the chamber. The chamber (now containing air at exactly the same pressure as the surroundings) was connected to a mouthpiece in the diver's mouth via a corrugated tube, thus the diver could easily breathe in; as he emptied the chamber of air the diaphragm was sucked into the 'open' position and air flowed freely. When the diver breathed out the air pressure inside the chamber rose. This moved the diaphragm into the central 'closed' position stopping the flow of air from the cylinder.

To enable the diver to get rid of his expired air a second tube was connected to the mouthpiece. This outlet tube was made of corrugated rubber, like the inlet tube, and was also connected to the valve on top of the air cylinder. It had a simple, duck-beak, non-return valve at the end of it, which was housed for protection inside a perforated metal chamber. This allowed the blown-out air to escape into the water, giving the characteristic plumes of bubbles now so familiar to all those who watch underwater films.

This new contraption, which enabled man to breath freely underwater with no connections to the surface, was called an *aqualung*. The heart of the new system was its revolutionary valve. Although various refinements have been made aqualungs still work on the same basic principle. The all important valves are sometimes referred to as regulators — because they 'regulate' the flow of air. They are also called demand valves because they provide air 'on demand'.

In Britain the new sport that evolved following the introduction of the aqualung was called, logically enough, *aqualung diving*. The Americans however, coined a new word, *scuba*, which is made up from the first letters of the words 'self contained breathing apparatus'.

Nowadays aqualung diving and scuba diving both have the same meaning, but at the time the aqualung was developed another underwater self-contained breathing apparatus (scuba) was already in existence; so the word scuba could have led to some confusion. The alternative system was the oxygen rebreathing apparatus which was developed for military purposes. It consisted of a rubberised canvas bag filled with oxygen from a small cylinder. A mouthpiece on a tube connected to the bag enabled the diver — who was called a frogman because of the shape of the fins he wore — to breathe oxygen straight from the bag. When he exhaled he blew back into the bag. The gases passed through a cannister of soda lime which absorbed the carbon dioxide.

There is one very serious drawback to the use of this type of equipment. Pure oxygen is poisonous when inhaled at high pressures. Nobody knows exactly why this is so, but it is a well established fact.

In this picture Wendy Dobbs wears an aqualung with a twin hose regulator. Air is delivered through one tube and the exhaust air is released into the sea through a one-way valve in the regulator at the top of the air cylinder.

Getting into the water from a large vessel

Some people are more vulnerable than others. Oxygen rebreathing equipment is still used by services personnel, but most navies limit its use to a maximum depth of 9 metres because of the hazard of oxygen poisoning. Most amateur diving clubs completely ban the use of oxygen rebreathing apparatus.

The next time you hear somebody refer to a diver as using oxygen from his aqualung, remember that he is technically wrong. Aqualung divers use air not oxygen.

Aqualung diving

As we have seen the aqualung consists of a cylinder of compressed air and a demand valve. The cylinders are known colloquially as bottles in Britain. They are also sometimes referred to as tanks, which is one of the words which has drifted across the Atlantic to join our diving language from the United States.

Although many divers still use and prefer twin-hose demand valves, single hose regulators are becoming increasingly popular. In the single-hose regulator there are two separate parts to the pressure reduction system. The first stage consists of a small valve attached to the neck of the cylinder. This reduces the pressure of the air which then passes along a narrow gauge tube to the mouthpiece. Another valve in the mouthpiece reduces the pressure still further and finely adjusts it so that it flows into the diver's lungs when he inhales. The expired air is blown out through the mouth. The bubbles are deflected away from the front of the mask so that they do not obscure the diver's vision.

You may conclude from this description that breathing from a demand valve requires skill. It doesn't, in practice it is unbelievably simple. You just put the mouthpiece in your mouth, a rubber flange slips between your lips and gums to form a seal; the mouthpiece is kept in place by gently biting on two rubber spigots. You just breathe in and out through your mouth. If you are wearing a facemask and submerge into a shallow pool you will detect no change in the easy breathing action.

The first 'bubble' with an aqualung is a tremendous sensation. No longer do you have to hold your breathe and then rush to the surface for air. You have your own personal supply neatly contained in a cylinder on your back. You are weightless and free as a fish to explore the mysterious world beneath the sea.

Getting in and swimming with an aqualung underwater is easy. I am tempted to say dead easy. Because it is equally important to come back out again — alive. To do that you must understand the limitations of your equipment and your body, and follow certain rules.

Embolism

The first rule applies in even shallow water and it is easy to observe. It is: *do not hold your breath and*

Aqualung divers examine and photograph a coral head.

An aqualung diver rolls backwards into the water from a small fishing boat.

rise quickly to the surface. If you do, the air inside your lungs, which is at the same pressure as the water all around you when you inhale, will expand. If it is not allowed to escape it may rupture the delicate tissues of the lungs, giving rise to what doctors call pulmonary pneumothorax. If some of the bubbles enter the arterial system and cause a blockage — known as an air embolism — the results could be fatal. You will not get an embolism if you continue to breathe in and out as you rise slowly to the surface. As a guide to your rate of ascent: do not rise faster than your smallest bubbles.

Air embolisms are very rare and most likely to occur with a novice diver who panics and races for the surface desperately holding his breath. If you have to make an emergency ascent, and there is not another diver nearby to share his air with you, then you must exhale as you swim to the surface. In practice, if you are aware of the hazard, it is possible to feel the build up of pressure in the lungs before it reaches danger level and you can let the excess air bleed gently from your mouth.

Ear clearing
If you have had a cold and blown your nose hard you may have felt your ears 'pop'. This happens when there is a sudden rush of air into the cavity behind the eardrum. A similar sensation may be experienced when diving.

When it is in its normal state the pressure is the same on both sides of the eardrum, but when the diver descends the pressure on the outside surface of the eardrum increases. This must be counter-balanced: air must flow from the throat into the cavity behind the eardrum until the pressure is again equal on both sides of the eardrum.

Always descend at such a rate that dangerous pressure differences — signalled by pain in the ears — do not develop. Some people experience very little difficulty with ear clearing. They pinch their noses and blow gently as they descend. Their ears click and they can dive safely at a very fast rate. Others, and I am unfortunately one of them, always have to descend very slowly. It is for this reason that I usually prefer to descend to the seabed down an anchor rope. If necessary I can cling to the line and wait until my ears click.

Ear plugs should never be worn by snorkel divers or by aqualung divers, because they prevent ear clearing by blocking the outside passage to the eardrum.

Nitrogen narcosis

The 'narcs' is the slang term given by divers to what is known technically as nitrogen narcosis. 'Rapture of the deep' is the more poetic term given to this condition.

Rapture of the deep is a good phrase because it describes the symptoms of a physiological pheno-menon that can occur when divers wearing aqualungs descend to depths in excess of 45 metres. We still do not know how it happens. What we do know is that the nitrogen in the inhaled air is responsible and that some people are more susceptible than others. When a person reaches his susceptible depth he starts to feel elated. He may behave as if he has been drinking and become irresponsible, and it is this irresponsibility that may lead to a fatal situation. It has been reported that a diver suffering from nitrogen narcosis wanted to give his mouthpiece to a passing fish!

Although being suspended in a euphoric underwater glow may be a pleasant way of departing this world for the next, it does leave those on the surface with unpleasant problems. One of the rules when diving deep is: *never dive alone and keep a careful watch on your diving companion.* If your partner shows any signs of irresponsibility, stop descending and make him rise. As soon as he rises above his susceptible depth he should become clear-minded again. It is also essential that you should be accompanied by an experienced diver on your first deep dive.

Bill Smith explains the working of the aqualung to Paddi Benson before her first sea dive off the coast of Mauritius.

Paddi Benson goes down the anchor rope to adventure. Her instructor wears an ABLJ.

A decompression table, clearly defining decompression stops, has been stuck on to a spare aqualung cylinder. It hangs on the decompression line during a deep dive off the coast of Sardinia.

The bends

The bends are so called because divers who suffer from them may become partially paralysed and walk with a bent stoop on land. Many of the early sponge divers in the Mediterranean suffered from the bends. They knew the bends were associated with deep diving, but did not know how to prevent them. They used to plummet to the sea bed in their cumbersome rubberised canvas suits and copper helmets. When they had collected a bag of sponges they would signal to the tender in the boat and be whisked to the surface. Usually nothing happened. Sometimes they got aches and pains in their joints and, after a while, the pain disappeared. At other times, when the pain subsided, they were left partially paralysed — or bent. In severe cases they died.

We now know that the bends are caused by excessive nitrogen dissolving in the blood under pressure. If the diver rises too rapidly to the surface the dissolved gas forms bubbles — like bubbles in an opened bottle of fizzy lemonade. The bubbles block the tiny blood vessels that supply the nervous system. Starved of oxygen the nerves cease to function properly and paralysis sets in. In the very severe cases large bubbles of nitrogen block major blood vessels and cause death.

Treatment for a person suffering from the bends is to recompress him as soon as possible. Recompression forces the bubbles to dissolve in the blood. The pressure is then slowly decreased at such a rate that the dissolved gas can be safely expelled through the lungs during respiration. Recompression can be achieved by sending a diver down again to a depth where the symptoms disappear and then bring him slowly to the surface. Alternatively, if the facility is available, he can be put into a recompression chamber. In the dry and warm he is recompressed and the air pressure reduced in stages.

Now that we understand why the bends occur, we can take steps to prevent them. After a deep descent, the return to the surface is carried out in a series of stages, the depths and timings of which are indicated in decompression tables.

It is essential for divers to become familiar with decompression tables during training. Divers who propose to go on deep dives should plan them carefully. They should carry sufficient air to allow them to make the necessary decompression stops as they return to the surface. They should also discover the whereabouts of the nearest decompression

The aqualung diver who goes below 9 metres may need to decompress on the way back to the surface. To do this he must have a reliable watch, a good depth gauge and a decompression table.

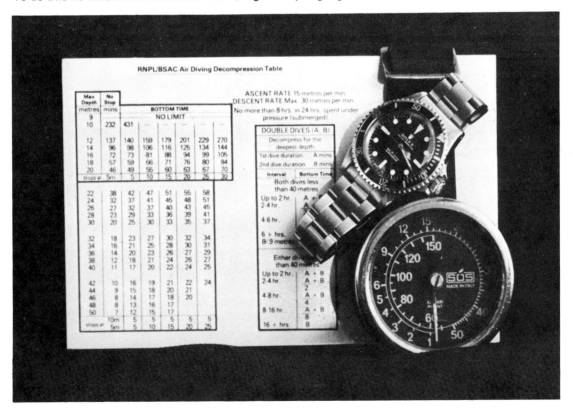

The cylinder hanging on the decompression line has a regulator with two take-offs on it: this is called an 'octopus rig'.

chamber.

Remember, the deeper you go and the longer you stay there the greater is the possible danger from the bends. If you are prepared to confine your diving to depths of less than 9 metres no decompression stops are required — regardless of how long you dive.

Cold and fatigue

Cold is an insidious hazard that lies in wait for the diver at all depths. It is possible to become so engrossed in your exploration of the underwater world, that you are unaware that you are becoming cold and that your energy is draining away.

Aqualung divers go deeper, where the water is colder, than snorkel divers. They also tend to swim more slowly and generate less heat, so aqualung divers need insulation more than snorkel divers.

I did not wear a wetsuit on my first dive in the

Mediterranean and I became very cold. I now regard at least a wetsuit jacket as essential when diving in the Mediterranean, a sea which most holiday makers would regard as comfortably warm.

As all forms of protective clothing, including wetsuits, are restrictive, the thickness and amount of clothing is kept to a minimum. However, the minimum thickness of a wetsuit that will keep you comfortable throughout a dive varies, not only with the water temperature, but also the depth. This is because the increased pressure compresses the tiny air bubbles trapped in the rubber of the suit material and its heat insulating property is reduced. By increasing the thickness of the sponge neoprene the heat loss is diminished. Because of this, suits are available in different thicknesses for various diving conditions.

Heat insulation requirements vary from person to person. Fat people, like seals, have a built-in layer which reduces heat loss. Thin people need extra protection. I am in the latter category and I find that, when diving off the British Coast, I am most comfortable wearing a suit of the thickest material available (7mm). Other divers find suits made of 5mm thick neoprene are adequate.

One part of the body that it is vital to keep warm is the head. As the blood supply to the head passes through the neck, that too should be kept well insulated. Ill fitting hoods over jackets with loose collars should be avoided. The best way to keep head and neck insulated is to wear a jacket with the hood attached. Bootees and fins should not be too tight or they will restrict circulation to the feet and become extremely uncomfortable.

Divers are continuously pushing forward the frontiers of their explorations. Visits are now regularly made to the cold world beneath the polar ice. To progress diving under such arduous conditions technology has been brought to the aid of the diver. The development of waterproof zip fasteners has led to the introduction of inflatable drysuits in which the volume of air inside the suit is maintained at depth by the introduction of more air. In this way a high degree of insulation is retained and the problem of the squeeze, encountered with the early dry suits, is eliminated. At present inflatable drysuits are more expensive than wetsuits; but as more and more people discover their higher comfort factor, they will be more widely used and, as the battle against the cold is won, the diving season will be extended.

Buoyancy control

The use of thick wetsuits at depth brings with it a problem of buoyancy control, for to be comfortable in the water the diver must be not only warm he must also be neutrally buoyant. A diver may need to wear a weightbelt with as much as 9 kilogrammes

Above *a good wetsuit will keep a diver warm even under the hardest conditions. This photograph was taken by Dave Gill under five feet of ice in Alaska. Inflatable drysuits are being used increasingly for cold water diving.* Below *a diver is photographed under the ice in Blenheim Lake.*

weight of lead on it to counteract the buoyancy of his suit on the surface. As he descends his suit becomes compressed and his buoyancy decreases. Thus less weight is required to obtain a state of neutral buoyancy at depth.

How can the diver overcome this problem?

He can estimate, from previous experience, the amount of weight he will require at his working depth so that he is not seriously overweight. This lower weight requirement will make him buoyant on the surface. It may be necessary for him to swim down hard, or pull himself down the anchor rope to overcome the initial buoyancy at the beginning of the dive. He must also remember that he will be positively buoyant near the surface at the end of the dive. This is particularly important if he proposes to make decompression stops. Some additional weights attached to the decompression shot line may be the solution in this situation.

Another way of solving the problem is for the diver to wear an ABLJ (adjustable buoyancy lifejacket). This is a lifejacket that can be inflated at depth from its own integral air cylinder, or via a connection to the aqualung, or both. The diver can put on sufficient weight to be neutrally buoyant on the surface, but as he gets deeper, and the buoyancy of his wetsuit decreases, he can 'trim off' his overall buoyancy by introducing the appropriate amount of air into his lifejacket. When he ascends the excess air is bled off via a valve incorporated into the ABLJ for the purpose. Pressure relief valves are also built into ABLJs to prevent them from bursting should they inadvertantly be over inflated.

The ABLJ can be a lifesaver, not just because it can keep an unconscious diver afloat on the surface, but because the extra air it contains may be sufficient to keep a submerged diver who is trapped alive for a few more vital minutes until help arrives. This was certainly the case for Ron Blake who was lost in an underwater cave at a depth of 110 feet off the Island of Zembra. The silt stirred up by the divers completely hid the entrance. Rather than swim aimlessly around in the pitch dark Ron decided to sit tight and wait for help. Showing incredible calm he waited in the dark. First his main air supply ran out, then his reserve. Still sitting tight he switched to breathing air from his ABLJ. He blew out one breath into the water and the next two or three breaths he blew back into the bag. Eventually he became unconscious and although he dislodged his facemask, he miraculously kept his mouthpiece in position. Reg Vallintine, now Director General of the British Sub-Aqua Club, made a dramatic eleventh hour rescue. He managed to haul Ron to the surface and resuscitate him before they both descended again to carry out their decompression schedule. Ron is only alive today because of his calm self control, plus the fact that he was wearing a newly acquired ABLJ.

The use of an ABLJ requires a thorough understanding of its working principles and the method of buoyancy adjustments should be well practiced before it is used on deep dives.

Left an adjustable buoyancy life jacket (ABLJ) with its air cylinder clearly visible at the bottom of the jacket. Right an ABLJ which has its integral air cylinder behind the front of the air sack.

Above *a training session in an open air pool.* Below *the first stage in learning to dive with an aqualung is to become familiar with all the equipment.*

Above left *fitting a mask underwater is one of the drills which must be mastered during a pool training session.* Above right *a pupil shares the air from her aqualung with an instructor who wears no breathing apparatus.* Below left *to clear your ears underwater you pinch your nose and blow.* Below right *a diver must be able to breathe from an aqualung underwater when he is not wearing a mask.*

Before he can be certified as Third Class, a diver must be able to fit all his equipment while at the bottom of a swimming pool.

Learning to dive with an aqualung

A good analogy between learning snorkel diving and aqualung diving is between riding a bicycle and driving a car. The techniques of snorkel diving, like riding a bicycle, can be picked-up with the minimum of assistance, although the pupil will obviously benefit from expert guidance. Aqualung diving is different. In the same way that I would not recommend anyone to drive a car without tuition, I do not think that anyone should venture into the sea with an aqualung without proper tuition.

There are a number of centres around Britain where, for a fee, you can undergo a course of training. Numerous holiday centres, such as the Forte Village in Sardinia, provide instruction in aqualung diving. In the United States of America there are hundreds of diving schools. The standard of training at different commercial organisations varies enormously.

The British Sub-Aqua Club (BSAC) is a governing body for sports diving. It has Branches in most of the large towns in Britain, as well as overseas. Its high standard of training is recognised throughout the diving world. Indeed, one of the foundation stones upon which the success of the BSAC has been built has been its aqualung diver training scheme. This is described in detail in the Club's Diving Manual, which is often referred to as the 'bible'. The widespread use of the BSAC Diving Manual for training amateur divers by organisations such as the Royal Navy, which are outside the BSAC, testifies to the soundness of the information it contains.

The basic premise upon which the BSAC training scheme is founded is that the newcomer to the sport should pass a logical succession of tests. The tests are based upon experience and are designed to give the trainee capability and confidence in the water. Members of a Branch of the BSAC receive a log book in which they record details of their training programme. There are several clearly defined milestones along the road, and when the pupil reaches a certain stage he can feel a sense of achievement as it is 'signed up' in his log book. He can then clearly see the next goal ahead, and train to achieve it.

It starts, as we have seen, with the attainment of the status of Snorkel Diver. By the time he has gained this qualification the diver should feel very at home in the water when wearing fins mask and snorkel. He should have no difficulty in progressing through the next series of tests to attain the status of 3rd Class Diver.

An understanding of at least the basic physics associated with taking the body underwater (such as that classic principle beloved of all science teachers — Boyle's Law) are necessary before a diver can fully appreciate the stresses he is likely to impose upon himself when he goes underwater. The diver should also be familiar with the basic physiology of respiration. These and other subjects are presented to the pupil in a series of lectures which usually run in parallel with training sessions in the swimming pool. At an inland Branch of the BSAC it may take six months or more for the newcomer to complete a gentle stepwise progression of lectures and pool training sessions before he dives with an aqualung in the sea.

The Group E Intermediate Aqualung Test which follows on from the Group D Snorkel Test is as follows:

1. Fit harness and demand valve to a cylinder. Test and put on cylinder.
2. Sink all equipment in the deep end of the pool. Dive and fit the equipment without surfacing.
3. Remove your mask underwater; replace and clear. Repeat three times.
4. Remove your mouthpiece underwater; replace and clear. Repeat three times.
5. Demonstrate mobility with an aqualung by completing three forward rolls and three backward rolls.
6. Demonstrate buoyancy control by adjusting your diving level by depth of respiration: breathe out hard, relax and lie on the bottom; lift off the bottom by controlled inspiration.
7. Fit a snorkel tube and remove an aqualung on the surface at the deep end of the pool; fin 50 metres towing an aqualung.

When a diver has been well trained he will find the experience of being weightless very relaxing.

Above *the weightless diver can easily perform somersaults underwater.* Below *a diver demonstrates buoyancy control: he adjusts the weights on his belt so that when he breathes in he rises gently and when he exhales he sinks.*

Many youngsters, quite naturally, want to learn to dive with an aqualung once they have mastered the techniques of snorkelling; but aqualung diving can be dangerous and children should only learn if their parents are active knowledgeable divers who can take full responsibility for them. The BSAC will not train divers who are under sixteen years old.

This is followed by the Group F Intermediate Aqualung Test:

1. Fin 100 metres on the surface as follows:
   50 metres alternating between a snorkel and an aqualung;
   50 metres on your back, wearing an aqualung and carrying a snorkel but using neither.
2. Surfacing drill: In the deep end of the pool, surface and remove your mouthpiece, fit a snorkel and give 'O.K.' signal. Repeat three times.
3. Share an aqualung with companion for 25 metres at a depth not exceeding 3 metres.
4. Fin 50 metres underwater with your mask blacked-out, led by a companion or following a rope.
5. Fin 50 metres submerged and at speed. Complete in the deep end of the pool where a companion is simulating insensibility. Release both weightbelts; bring the 'body' to the surface and tow it for 25 metres by the BSAC method incorporating EAR. Remove both sets of equipment in the water; land the 'body' (assistance is permitted), and carry out EAR.
6. Dismantle, clean and dry an aqualung, and stow it away to the Instructor's satisfaction.

The author takes one of his pupils on her first sea dive in the Indian Ocean.

It is vital to learn the basic signs for communicating underwater. This sign means 'are you OK?' and also 'yes, I am OK'.

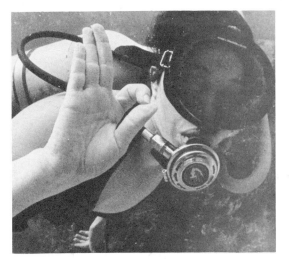

On completion of Groups E and F tests, the pupil may, at the discretion of the Branch Diving Officer, progress to open water aqualung training. He will then take the Group G test:

1. Demonstrate in open water while wearing an aqualung, the surfacing drill and diver-to-surface-party signals.
2. Demonstrate in open water while wearing an aqualung, the correct adjustment of buoyancy when wearing a diving suit.
3. Carry out at least five open water dives to a depth of not less than 7 metres, and for submerged durations of not less than 15 minutes each. A diving suit must be worn for at least one of these dives.
4. On one open water dive, 'rescue' an aqualung diver; tow the 'body' 50 metres using the BSAC method incorporating EAR (another diver may assist).

Each time a trainee attends one of the compulsory lectures, or completes one of his qualifying dives, he records it in his 'Qualification Record' (a booklet which doubles as a diving log) and has it signed by the instructor.

When all of his lectures and qualifying dives have been 'signed up' the trainee will have to take an appropriate theory test set by the Branch Diving Officer. Once he has done that he may be rated by the Branch Committee as a *Third Class Diver*. His Qualification Record will be stamped and signed.

Many divers are satisfied when they reach Third Class Diver standard. For the ambitious diver, however, there are further goals. The next step in the progression is to *Second Class Diver*. Ultimately there is *First Class Diver* which, among other things, requires that the applicant should have logged at least one hundred open water dives and passed a comprehensive written and practical examination.

A diver's Qualification Record is very

Aqualung diving in the kelp jungle off Fort Bovisand in Devon

important to him if he wishes to go diving with people who do not know, from first hand experience, his diving ability. Suppose, for example he goes on holiday, and wants to join a diving expedition. How does the expedition leader assess the risk he is taking by allowing a stranger to dive? If the person who wishes to join can produce his Qualification Record the expedition leader can see in a moment the level to which this potential member of his diving team has been trained. The moral here is, always take your Qualification Record with you when you travel to a place where you may be able to dive, even if you have no specific plans to do so.

The organization which regulates the standard of diving sports on a world-wide basis is the Confederation Mondiale des Activites Subaquatiques which is generally referred to by its initials CMAS, (pronounced 'sea mass'). CMAS have devised a star system of diver qualification which relates to the BSAC scheme approximately as follows:

one star	: pool training only, no sea dives
two star	: Third Class Diver
three star	: Second Class Diver
four star	: First Class Diver

Members of the British Sub-Aqua Club can apply to Headquarters for the appropriate CMAS Star Certificate if they are travelling to a part of the world where such a certificate is the only acceptable diving qualification.

The end of training — what next?

For many divers the attainment of 3rd Class Diver status may appear to be the end of the line. The reason for this is that a number of diving clubs concentrate so hard on the admittedly all important need for training, that they neglect the follow-up activities. But the end of training should really be the beginning of new and absorbing diving interests. If these are not provided then trained members tend to drift away. There is absolutely no reason why this should happen. Nobody should be deterred from starting a project because he does not think the members of his club will have the necessary skills. For one characteristic of every diving club that I know is that the members are a miscellaneous bunch. I have yet to discover a club that could not undertake any reasonable (and some quite unreasonable) project.

For me learning to dive was like finding the key to a treasure house of new and exciting interests. After nearly twenty years those interests are still expanding and are as captivating as ever.

Only very experienced divers should dive in caves and all cave dives should be thoroughly planned in advance. Cave diving in clear water among stalactites and stalagmites can be a wonderful experience, as the author discovered when diving in the Crystal Caves of Bermuda.

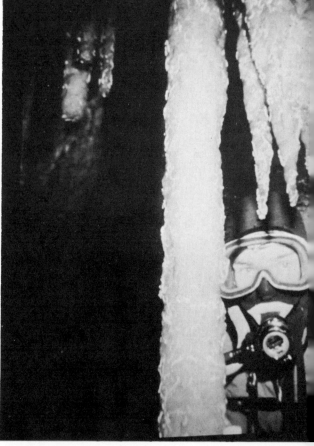

Brightly coloured creatures can often be found in underwater caves. Why they have such vivid colours when they live in an environment without light is one of the many mysteries of the sea.

Underwater Photography

The pioneers of underwater photography were faced with many problems that have now been largely resolved. The first of these was the problem of actually getting their cameras into the water. They put standard above water cameras in waterproof and pressure resistant boxes. A camera lens would 'look' through a glass window sealed into one box. The camera controls were operated via control rods that passed through watertight glands. Many ingenious methods were devised which enabled the simple rotational movements of the knobs on the outside of a housing to operate the delicate and often intricate actions of the camera controls inside.

Camera housings were designed and built from a variety of materials. Some designers started with pre-fabricated containers. These varied from fuse boxes to pressure cookers. Others started from scratch using metal plates which were cut and welded together to form the basic box unit of the housing. Nowadays commercial housings are available; but with so many people interested in DIY many cameras still go underwater in home made cases. Perspex is the material most widely used by the DIY enthusiasts.

For those who now wish to buy a camera housing there is a wide selection to choose from. The Rolls Royce of still cameras is the Hassleblad. A Hassleblad with accessories, including underwater housings, could cost a thousand pounds. The amateur divers who use Hassleblads for their underwater pictures are an exclusive band. At the other end of the price scale is the Kodak Instamatic. It is possible to purchase, relatively

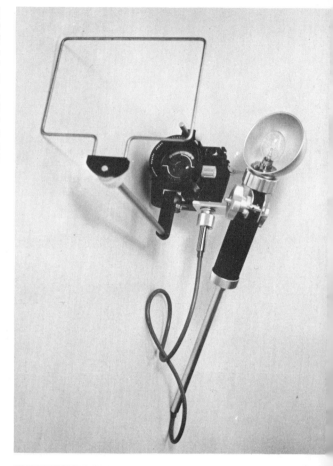

Below the most widely used underwater camera is the Nikonos. Above right the Nikonos, complete with flash, close-up lens and a frame showing the field of view; Right the Nikonos fitted with a fish-eye supplementary lens and viewfinder. With these attachments clear pictures can be taken in murky water.

Jill Myers, of the Norfed Photographic Society, 'shoots' a fish in the Indian Ocean, with her Nikonos camera plus electronic flash.

cheaply, a simple moulded plastic housing for such cameras.

A major advance in underwater photography was made with the introduction of the first camera designed specifically for underwater use. It was called the Calypso-phot and has since been up-dated and renamed the Nikonos. Such cameras are called amphibious cameras because they can be used above water and below water without modification.

Another amphibious camera sold in Britain is the Anfibian. It is a 35mm snapshot camera with a single fixed shutter speed and aperture. It is sold complete with flash which is necessary for most underwater subjects.

The most popular amphibious still camera used throughout the world today is the Nikonos, which is manufactured by the Japanese company of Nikon. The Nikonos is a precision-made 35mm camera with all three controls (shutter speed, aperture and focus) that you would find on an equivalent high quality

land camera. The standard lens is sealed in air behind a flat glass porthole, which is a bayonet fit into the camera body. When the lens is in position the third major component, the film transport system and the focal plane shutter, is locked into position. Watertight seals are achieved throughout with rubber 'O' rings.

The Nikonos is a remarkable little camera, for it is no bigger than a conventional 35mm camera, yet it can be used above water, or below water to a depth of 45 metres. It is the basic unit in an underwater photographic system that has been steadily enlarged since the camera was first introduced. Nikon make a number of accessories, which range from a selection of alternative lenses to a bulb flashgun. Because of its popularity, other manufacturers also produce accessories specifically for the Nikonos. This expands the use of the camera to cover virtually all of the situations where a skin diver is likely to want to take pictures.

The Ricoh 35 mm camera can be fitted into a commercially made plastic housing.

Stills photography

One of the problems of underwater photography is the relatively low visibility. An underwater visibility of 30 metres is exceptionally good. The underwater photographer must get as close to his subject as possible to reduce the effects of the underwater fog to a minimum. If he wishes to photograph a large subject, or a group of divers, his camera must 'see' a large field of view. This is possible only if he uses a so-called *wide angle lens.* The ultimate wide angle lens, the *fish-eye lens* can 'see' through an angle of nearly 180°. A true fish eye lens produces a circular image on the film and the figures at the edge of the image are very distorted. Such pictures have a limited appeal and many photographers opt for a compromise and use a *semi-fish-eye lens* which produces only a small degree of edge distortion, but still retains a wide angle view. The most popular method of taking wide angle pictures is to use a supplementary lens which can be fitted and removed from the camera underwater.

An alternative to the fish-eye lens for a completely different type of photography is the close-up lens. This again can be of the supplementary kind which is clipped on the front of the Nikonos camera. Close-up photography is certainly a most rewarding field for the photographer who is working off the British Coast. Close-up lenses are usually used in conjunction with flash and colour film. The flash puts back the red components of the natural light that are filtered out of normal daylight during its passage

Above *Geoff Harwood with his wide-angle supplementary lenses, called 'Vizmasters', which he has developed for the Nikonos camera. Below a picture taken on a night dive off Flamborough Head in Yorkshire.*

through water.

Flash close-up pictures are often brighter and more colourful than the actual subject as seen by the diver. When a small area of the seabed is photographed and the resultant transparency is projected the picture may be startlingly brilliant. The viewer may well see much more than he did when he was fleetingly looking at the live scene. The eye of the camera can reveal a wealth of marine life that the diver can inspect at his leisure. By doing this he will find that on future dives he will see much more because he has become aware of what there is to see.

Cinematography

Skin diving undoubtedly owes a lot of its popularity to film. For film, more than any other medium, can capture the thrill and pleasure of diving. It is film that has brought the underwater world into millions of homes through the medium of television.

Most television features are shot on 16mm film which is the same size as the film used for film shows in schools. This is much narrower than the 35mm and 70mm film used in large cinemas. The people who handle these professional, large formats refer to the very narrow gauge 8mm film used by amateurs as 'bootlace' film. 'Bootlace' or not, I think the use of 8mm film is an ideal way for the amateur to begin underwater film-making.

I would advise the amateur underwater film-maker

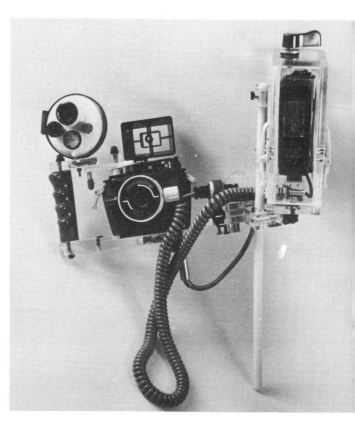

The Anfibian amphibious snapshot camera complete with flashgun

Above *the Nikonos camera and the Dobbs/ Aquamatic assembly which includes, electronic flash, exposure meter and one handed camera operation.* Below *the Ikelite housing for SLR cameras can be connected to a separate housing for an electronic flashgun.*

The camera takes a partial fish-eye view of divers on a coral reef in the Indian Ocean. The fish-eye lens is the ultimate wide-angle lens, it can 'see' through an angle of nearly 180°. A true fish-eye lens produces a circular image on the film and the figures at the edge of the image are very distorted.

Above a photographer, Dr Luciano Manara, descends into the clear waters of the Mediterranean. Below a problem for the photographer: should he let the crab go or should he take more pictures?

An easy way to start making underwater films is to use an 8 mm cine camera.

A fish-eye view of the author with the 16 mm camera housing which he built himself and uses for making films for television.

to use a Super-8mm camera with a wide angle lens. The depth of field is so great with wide angle lenses for 8mm cameras that a fixed focus lens is adequate for most purposes. You can forget about zoom or, if you have it, set it on maximum view. Automatic cine cameras are much easier to use, so in addition I would recommend electric motor drive and automatic exposure control, thus all that you need in the camera housing is one control — the shutter release.

When using a cine camera remember to keep all camera movements steady. As a general rule the cine camera should be moved for shots of still subjects but should be kept still when there is plenty of action. There are many exceptions to this rule, but

one of the commonest mistakes made by beginners is to constantly move the camera. Another mistake is to make sequences too short. Dozens of short 'squirt' shots with the camera and the subject moving are very hard on the eyes of the viewer, so keep at least some shots long. These can be location shots where the cameraman is setting up scene for the viewer. Such a shot can be what is called a 'dolly' where the cameraman swings slowly forward with the camera running, thereby giving the person watching the film the impression that he, or she, is finning over the seabed, or over a wreck.

An underwater movie should tell a story, even if it is simply the story of your holiday. It is certainly

advisable to plan the story you want to tell before you start filming, and to ask your fellow divers to co-operate in advance.

You can learn a lot by watching television films with a critical eye. Many apparently spontaneous shots are set up beforehand. See if you can spot them. Notice how frequently the cameraman changes his viewpoint and how this can change the mood of the sequence. For instance a head-on view of a diver working will keep the pace of a film steady. But tension can be heightened immediately if the camera swings under the divers and they are shown sillhouetted against the surface of the sea.

Remember that once you are in the water you will only be able to communicate with your 'actors' by hand signals, or with the simplest of written messages. So make sure that everyone knows exactly what you want them to do before you go overboard. However, be flexible. Do not become too obsessed with sticking to your preconceived story line. If something unusual happens, and it often does underwater, film it. It may never happen again. You can worry later about bending the story line to include the incident.

Editing is the name given to the process of knocking the film into its final shape and joining the different sequences together to make the story. The bridge between one situation and another can be made with a 'cutaway' shot — of almost any subject, usually in close-up — that is only loosely related to two separated shots. A cutaway shot can be the sea foaming over the rocks, a seagull, a diver's bubbles — almost anything.

Editing a film is as important as shooting the film. When editing a film remember: don't bore your audience; keep it short; always leave your audience wanting more.

Film making is concerned with creating illusions. The viewer should forget that he is sitting in front of a screen and feel that he is actually swimming with you as you explore the underwater world. With the sound of music to drown distractions such as the clatter of the projector, it is possible to ease the viewer gently into your world of inner space.

Horace Dobbs, the author of this book, has also written a comprehensive guide to practical underwater photography and film-making. It is called Camera Underwater *and is published by the Focal Press.*

A fish-eye view of the author filming with the Imperial Iranian Navy during a photography course at Fort Bovisand in Devon.

The Editor of Photography, *John Sanders, reads his own magazine 'in depth'.*

Treasure Hunting and Underwater Archaeology

One image of the skindiver is that of an adventurer searching for treasure on the seabed. Sometimes a diver really does find treasure. Kip Wagner found a Spanish dubloon when he was idly beach-combing in Florida in 1955. His find sparked off a treasure hunt that was at times more exciting than many of the fictional tales told about such treasure trails. On one outstanding day Kip Wagner uncovered a cache of coins valued at about one million dollars. By 1970, Wagner and his team were reported to have recovered treasure worth six million five hundred thousand dollars.

In the course of history virtually all of the major maritime nations have lost ships at sea. Many were wrecked around the treacherous shores of the British Isles. With a few notable exceptions, however, the chances of finding treasure around our shores were considered too small to warrant the effort of a treasure hunt. Very little serious treasure diving was done until the mid-nineteen sixties; then in 1967 the Navy Air Command Sub-Aqua Club discovered some cannon belonging to the *Association* between the Gilstone Rock and Gilstone Ledge off the Scilly Isles.

In 1707, a great fleet of British warships, under the command of Sir Cloudesley Shovell, foundered in the English Channel. The fleet had been campaigning in the Mediterranean and was carrying a cargo of gold and silver. The disaster took place 28 miles from Lands End at a place given the appropriate colloquial name of the Ships' Graveyard.

With the discovery of the *Association,* divers flocked to the Scillies like gold miners to the Klondike. The Ministry of Defence made the colossal bureaucratic blunder of giving three separate contracts permitting each holder to salvage the wreck. This led to a gigantic free-for-all scramble for treasure. Rivalry between different groups reached fever pitch. Diving safety standards were cast aside and it was reported that pitched battles took place underwater.

People concerned with the historic value of wrecks were horrified at what they termed the 'Rape of the *Association*'. To them the indiscriminate plundering of the wreck represented a loss far beyond that of the gold and silver coins spirited away

Pottery, such as this Roman amphora, may lie undiscovered on the seabed for hundreds of years. (Photograph by J. Morey Gil)

by the divers. It was the loss of information concerning a piece of history that could never be recovered. Their voice was heard. New legislation was introduced to prevent the recurrence of such a situation.

There are many gaps in our knowledge of old vessels and the way of life of the men who sailed them. A ship at sea is a self-contained community. When a ship founders the way of life of that community is frozen in time; but the picture is broken up, like the pieces of a jigsaw, and scattered over the seabed. Archeologists try to put the jigsaw together.

Today, if a diver discovers a wreck he is obliged, by British law, to do nothing unless he raises something from it. If he is wise he will keep quiet until he has had a chance to do some research, and perhaps to carry out a preliminary survey and to photograph the site. He will then need to raise at least one object that will enable him positively to identify what he has found. This object must be handed to the Receiver of Wreck who will see that it is inspected by the appropriate authorities. If the raised article is found to have come from a site of significant historic interest under the Wreck Protection Act the finder may be granted an exclusive licence to excavate the site. However, he will only be granted such a licence if he can convince the authorities that he proposes to carry out his excavations and salvage in a manner approved by the archeologists.

Many historic wrecks have been discovered by

Two large snoek guard the wreck of the SS Brentwood which lies on the seabed on the Florida Keys.

accident. All divers should be alert to the possibility that on one of their dives they may stumble across the site of valuable wreck. Indeed, wrecks are still being discovered in areas that have been frequented by divers for years. A wealth of marine growth quickly camouflages anything dumped into the sea, and unless you know what to look for you could quite easily swim right over a fortune and not be aware that it is there.

The first sign that you are likely to see of an ancient wreck off the British Coast is a cannon. It is likely to be close to land. Few ships sank in the open sea, most of them were driven on to the rocks in bad weather. With their hulls ripped open the unfortunate vessels would heel over spilling their guns on to the seabed where, because of their great weight, they would remain unmoved. The rigging and superstructure would be swept away by the sea as the hull sank and settled on the bottom. The keel and parts of the hull would gradually be enveloped in the ever shifting sand. The cargo and personal possessions of the luckless sailors would be scattered and disappear. Exposed surfaces of bare metal would provide a rare virgin surface where planktonic forms of marine life could settle and grow. Exposed wreckage would gradually become part of the changing scenery of the underwater world.

Iron cannons become covered in a steadily growing burden of concretion. The overall shape is retained but the outline is softened, often almost into unrecognition. Copper, however, is poisonous to marine organisms, so a bronze cannon may remain virtually devoid of marine growth and be easily recognised. This is why the first discovery on many wreck sites has been the finding of a bronze cannon.

This was certainly the case with the site of the *Trinidad Valencera.* Members of the City of Derry Branch of the British Sub-Aqua Club discovered this

A diver, from the Torbay Branch of the BSAC, probes the kelp covered wreck of the SS Jebba *which foundered on the rocks near Bolt Tail in Devon in 1907.*

wreck, quite by accident, off the Coast of Ireland during a routine winter dive in Kinnigoe Bay in February 1973. Can you imagine the excitement of making such a find? An escutchion, on one huge bronze cannon that they found, bore the coat of arms of the King of Spain, leaving no doubt as to the identity of the wreck they had discovered.

As nobody in the club had any previous knowledge of nautical archeology, they made contact with Colin Martin, founder of the St Andrew's Institute of Maritime Archeology in Scotland. Colin Martin advised them what to do and personally supervised what has since become a classic underwater archeological investigation.

When the wreck was first discovered one of the divers, Stan Donoghue telephoned Kendall MacDonald of the British Sub-Aqua Club and asked for advice and financial help. Kendall MacDonald contacted his friend the late Paul Johnstone of BBC Television, and suggested that the *Trinidad Valencera* might make a good subject for the 'Chronicle' series of documentary films. As a result the first stage of the archaeological study of the wreck was partially financed by the BBC, and a superb film record of the remarkable work done by

removed. Such a procedure is important because the information may reveal how the ship went down and give clues as to the likely whereabouts of other pieces of the wreck and its contents.

Once the survey had been carried out the team were free to raise the objects and lumps of concretion (each clearly identified with its number tag). The lumps of concretion known to contain metal were carefully examined on the surface, then the concretion was fractured and chipped away, and objects, that had last been used aboard that fateful galleon centuries before, again saw the light of day.

In addition to finding metal objects the divers also discovered a number of other artefacts which should have long since disintegrated and disappeared. A

Divers clear away the undergrowth of weed during a survey.

A diver rises through the hold of the wreck of the U.S. Liberty Ship James Eagen Layne *which lies in Whitesand Bay, Cornwall at a depth of about 20 metres.*

the divers was produced and shown on television. (A copy of the film is available from the BSAC.) One point that comes over very forcefully in the film is the enormous restraint and responsibility shown by the divers. There was no hint of gold fever. I doubt if any team of professional archaeologists could have been more dedicated and painstaking than this club of amateur divers.

Having raised the bronze cannon and thereby positively identified their find, the divers carried out a complete survey of the site. This was performed in much the same way that a survey would have been conducted on land. The seabed was divided into a grid with some key reference points such as outcrops of rock. A metal detector was used to find objects buried in the sand. A complete photographic record was taken and individual items were identified with numbered marker tags. Thus a complete picture of the site was built up before a single further object was

pair of fire bellows and a large wooden platter were recovered from the sand in near perfect condition — although the wooden parts had been reduced to the consistency of soggy cardboard.

Objects that have been preserved for centuries in the sea may disintegrate in a very short time on exposure to air. Thus in addition to surveying the site and raising the objects it was necessary to put a conservation programme in hand so that the treasure could be preserved and eventually put into a museum. Everyone agreed there was no point in raising more objects from the seabed (where they could safely remain for a further hundred years without deterioration) to quickly rot on the surface.

In three years the divers of the City of Derry Sub-Aqua Club only scratched the surface of their wreck. What still lies beneath the surface waiting to be discovered no one knows.

Underwater archeology is not confined exclusively to wrecks. In the Mediterranean and elsewhere surveys have been carried out, of ancient ports that were at one time on the land and now lie submerged beneath the sea.

The exploration of a well may reveal artefacts that

When a wreck is discovered, one of the first jobs is to measure and record all the objects before they are removed from the seabed.

span hundreds, or even thousands, of years. One of the most spectacular of such underwater explorations was carried out in the heart of the jungle in the Yucatan, at Chichen Itza, a centre of the Maya Civilization. The Maya Indians brought their human sacrifices to the well. Draped backwards over the arched altar stone, men women and children, stripped of their clothes were ceremoniously killed. The bodies were pushed over the cliff to drop 20 metres into the water below. Some of them remained undisturbed and preserved in the turbid water for 1500 years before being discovered, together with many artefacts, by the divers of the expedition.

Members of the Watford Underwater Club have carried out some very thorough underwater searches in wells in Hertfordshire. One of the ancient wells they have explored is at Chenies Manor. The well is 50 metres deep. The project, which was meticulously carried out over a period of more than a year, involved removing many tons of sludge, bucketful by bucketful, from the bottom of the well. Now that it has been cleared, the owner has converted the housing over the well into a little museum to contain some of the objects discovered by the divers.

On a wreck site off the British coast an overgrowth of seaweed may hide many artifacts.

The Underwater Naturalist

Fish-watching

Most newcomers to diving concentrate so hard on the mastery of their new found skills, and on enjoying the sheer exhiliration of being underwater that they see little of the natural life around them. They see the general pattern of the underwater world, but the detail escapes them. As they become more experienced and relaxed they see more and more.

Fish types and populations vary enormously according to local conditions. The most abundant and colourful fish life is undoubtedly to be found on a coral reef. Diving on a coral reef is an unforgettable experience. It is something really worth saving up for.

On a coral reef, in unpolluted waters, you will see fish in a variety and profusion that you have never seen before. Many of them are highly coloured and

The fish-watcher must always make a careful approach or the fish will flee.

Above *damsel fish find safety swimming among the heads of staghorn coral. This picture was taken by Keith Gillet off the Great Barrier Reef, Australia.* Below *the puffer fish is well camouflaged and blends in with its coral environment as shown in this photograph by Andre de Bloos.*

Above *a skindiver swoops down into the corals off the Coast of Bermuda.* Below *where there is a thriving colony of corals there is always plenty of fish life.*

weave in and out of the coral heads in a continuous gentle underwater ballet. The angel fish and butterfly fish are typical of the exotically coloured species you can see individually, or in twos and threes. Other fish such as the porkfish and grunts — so called because of their habit of grunting when caught — may be encountered in shoals of perhaps a hundred or more.

Such fish are easy to see and identify, but the thing that maintains a person's interest in fish-watching is the challenge of finding, recognising and perhaps photographing the more elusive species. The large batfish that float like sheets of chiffon in the shade of the coral are relatively easy to spot, but you may have to look hard to find a trumpet fish. This is a very attractive fish; and it is well camouflaged: you may find it in a head of coral pretending to be a coral branch.

Underwater scenery and fish life vary according to the part of the world where they are found. A rocky, or coral region has a different fish population to that found on and over a flat sandy seabed. Different species of fish have, during the course of evolution, acquired different shapes, colours and defence mechanisms; and fish tend to remain in the location to which they are best adapted to feed and flourish. The flatfish are a typical and well known example. They live and feed on the flat sandy areas of the seabed. Their undersides are white, and they are difficult to see from underneath because they blend so well with the bright surface of the sea. Likewise their topsides are brown and mottled to blend with the seabed, which makes them difficult to spot from above. Some flatfish make even greater efforts to camouflage their presence. They lie flat on the seabed and fluff sand over their bodies until just their eyes protrude. They remain quite still and nine out of ten novice divers will swim right over these fish and be quite unaware of their presence. The experienced fish-watcher, however, will notice the irregularity in the pattern of the seabed. When the fish knows the game is up it will take flight and flutter gracefully, but hastily away, shedding its covering of sand as it goes.

Some reef dwellers spend most of their time in one hole, which is their own underwater house. Typical of such fish is the blennie family. The blennies are popular with fish-watchers because they have endearing characters and can be found in easily accessible sites in shallow water. One of my favourites is the tompot blennie. It is about four inches long and has two feathery tufts on its head that look like bushy eyebrows. The tompot uses its pelvic fins like legs and spends most of its time propped up on them on its front doorstep watching the world go by with its bright eyes.

In addition to making their homes in the natural crevices in the rocks the hole dwellers will take up residence in any suitable man-made object that comes their way. So if you see an old pot or pipe on

Above *some fish stand out brilliantly against the coral background. They seem to be saying 'look out I am dangerous'. This is true of a family of fish known variously as lion fish, turkey fish, fire fish or sun fish. All these fish have poisonous spines which they display when danger threatens. Below the large spots on the tails of these butterfly fish from Bermuda may represent eyes and confuse predators.*

A coral reef has an infinite variety of textures and shapes. This coral seascape is in the Florida Keys.

the seabed take a quiet look inside. You may see two bright eyes looking out at you. They could belong to a small octopus or a blennie. The next step is to see if you have skill and patience enough to entice the animal out of its home.

Some fish forms are as bizarre as they are fascinating. Why did Nature produce that charming little chap, the sea horse? You might well find one of his relatives — the pipe fish — among the rocks, in shallow water off the British Coast. The male fish has a kangaroo-like feature: a small pouch on its abdomen in which it keeps fertilised eggs until they hatch.

The naturalist may occasionally see an octopus off the British Coast, but he is much more likely to do so in a rocky region of the Mediterranean. The octopus has a wonderful chameleon-like ability to change its colour to merge with its surroundings. It can also change the texture of its skin to make detection even more difficult. The octopus has a quite unjustified reputation for being dangerous, probably because of its somewhat fearsome appearance. When disturbed the octopus takes flight in a series of jet-propelled jerks. When pursued it squirts out clouds of dark brown ink.

Conservation

In some parts of the world pressures have been put on the natural resources of the underwater world to such an extent that it has been necessary to introduce conservation measures. The threats have come from many sources; pollution is one and overfishing by commercial fishermen is another. Also the divers themselves have contributed to the destruction of the very world they love.

In some parts of the Mediterranean the water is

This sea whip coral may look like a plant, but in fact it is a colony of microscopic animals.

This moorish idol is one of many fish that a diver may see when he swims over a shallow coral reef.

very clear and has been intensely spearfished for many years. In such regions it is unusual for a diver to see any of the large fish which were reported by the early underwater explorers to be present in considerable numbers. Territorial fish such as the grouper take many years to grow to full size and they fall easy prey to the speargun. Those that have not been killed have taken refuge in deep water, well out of range of the diver.

The beautiful deep pink gorgonian coral, found off the south west coast of England, grows at the rate of only one centimetre per year. With a quick flick of his knife a diver can destroy a growth that took fifty years to reach its full majesty.

The sea can no longer be regarded as a place where everyone can take as much as he wants, as often as he wants, without ill effects. Many divers now voluntarily restrict their souvenir taking to an absolute minimum. They no longer shoot with a speargun. They shoot with a camera instead. Thus they leave the creatures they 'shoot' to be seen and enjoyed by those who come afterwards.

Above *a diver prises a sea urchin from the rocks at Cape Spartivento in Sardinia. The damsel fish that surround him are sometimes known as 'flies of the sea'.* Left *a diver captures an octopus during a dive off the coast of Sardinia.*

Above left *edible crabs live in rocky areas around the British coast.* Above right *the pipefish is a charming and harmless little fish. This one was photographed at Fort Bovisand in Devon.* Below *along the coast of the Mediterranean, sea creatures have learned to be wary of divers. This octopus was caught by the flash from an underwater camera during a night dive.*

Above left *the peacock worm looks like a flower but in fact it is an animal that filters plankton from the seawater.* Above right *the tompot blennie can be found peering from crevices in rocks and harbour walls around much of the British coast.* Below *'on guard': a diver has a duel with a spider crab off the Devonshire coast.*

Underwater photography has revealed that life exists in the deeper parts of the ocean. This photograph was taken, using a remote control camera, at a depth of 800 metres by Professor Harold Egerton of the Massachusetts Institute of Technology.

Diving Holidays

Holidays in Britain

There are plenty of areas around the British Coast that are good centres for a diving holiday. As a general rule the West Coast is better than the East Coast. Many of the best diving sites are offshore and can only be reached by boat. It is therefore worth browsing through the advertisements in the diving journals to gather information about places that cater specifically for divers and also provide boats.

One of the most popular diving areas in the country is the coastline of Dorset, Devon and Cornwall. Visibility in the English Channel is usually better than it is in the Bristol Channel so the south coast is more popular. Plymouth is a good choice for a diving holiday. It offers a good variety of activities for non-divers, or for those days when diving has to be abandoned. The Marine Biological Station on the Hoe has an excellent aquarium where fish can be

For reasons of safety divers usually stay in groups of two or three. In this photograph two groups of divers met up during a diving holiday in the Indian Ocean.

studied at leisure. There are plenty of boats for hire. The nearby Underwater Centre at Fort Bovisand is always a hive of activity. There are lectures on many aspects of the underwater world, provided by well known speakers, throughout the year. One of the old gun emplacements has been converted into a bar with an unsurpassed view over Plymouth Sound.

If you like Devon and Cornwall but don't like the crowds, then the Isle of Man is well worth your consideration. The Isle of Man sits in the Gulf Steam and its waters are relatively warm and clear. If you are taken to the right spots you will see some of the most beautiful underwater scenery to be found anywhere off the British Coast.

The deep lochs of the west coast of Scotland are renowned for their clear, calm water and interesting dives, so too are the offshore islands although the weather out to sea is always unpredictable. This area is still relatively little visited by divers although the local Scottish divers are active throughout the year. The newly established school for training professional divers at Fort William may focus more attention on this area of Britain as a holiday centre.

Diving off the British Coast calls for a high level of diving expertise. Offshore dives should, whenever possible, be carried out with a boatman experienced in the ways and needs of divers. Tide tables should always be consulted and dives timed to coincide with slack water.

There are branches of the British Sub-Aqua Club throughout Britain and most of them welcome

Inflatable boats are very popular with divers, but journeys can be very bumpy if the sea is even slightly rough, so it is important to stow equipment carefully.

visitors. Contact with a local diving club at a holiday location can save a lot of time and trouble. They know where the best diving sites are and, more importantly, they know the areas where the tide can be treacherous for the diver diving from the beach. The local diving club will probably be able to help you with supplies of air, and will be able to advise on boats etc. A list of Branches of the BSAC which includes the names and addresses of the secretaries is available from Headquarters.

The Mediterranean

In many ways diving in the Mediterranean is much easier than it is off the British Coast. The water is clearer and warmer. Also there is little tide. This does not mean that currents do not exist; they do, and the diver should be alert for them.

The clear water in the Mediterranean seems to reduce the impression of depth. When you are on the sea bed 30 metres down and look up to see the boat clearly suspended on the surface, the height of the water above you seems far less than it does when you are 30 metres down in murky water. This illusion of shallowness, coupled with the fact that time can pass very quickly when you are enjoying yourself on a dive, can create a situation in which you may be unaware of the need to decompress on your way back to the surface, and you could be running into the dangerous possibility of suffering a bend, so beware: take a depth gauge, watch and decompression table with you; remember also, that you need a supply of air to decompress, don't wait until your air has nearly run out before starting the ascent.

There are many centres scattered throughout the Mediterranean where diving equipment can be hired and cylinders recharged. The breathing quality of the air supplied and the type and condition of gear for hire varies considerably from place to place. Information from divers who have already visited a centre is always useful, both for their impressions of the diving itself and the facilities available.

Turtles are quite harmless and will sometimes tow a diver along. Divers encountered this turtle off Malindi in Kenya.

The snorkeller finds a diving paradise off the coast of Mauritius — a calm shallow lagoon, full of fish and coral, and protected by a fringing coral reef 300 metres offshore.

Where the trade winds blow

If you want to see fish life in undreamed of profusion and an underwater world more picturesque than anything you can see in the Mediterranean, you must travel to the regions of the world where the trade winds blow. For it is only in these regions that the water remains warm enough throughout the year to maintain the growth of tropical corals.

The accessibility of coral reefs to divers varies considerably in different parts of the world. On island sites the reef may be separated from the island by a lagoon. In parts of Bermuda the reef is as far as 16 kilometres offshore. This increases the complexity of a dive and makes a boat essential — which in turn increases the cost. The snorkellers and inexperienced divers can dive in safety on the lagoon side of a fringing reef. The outer edge of the reef will attract the experienced divers. The reef often drops steeply to considerable depths. Such sites are known appropriately as 'drop offs'. It is here that the water is likely to be clear, the underwater scenery at its most spectacular, and it is here that the diver is likely to encounter large fish, and other species such as turtles.

In regions where there is a fringing reef the sea can become quite rough if the wind blows strongly. If the wind is onshore it can send the sea pounding over the reef. In such conditions the underwater visibility can be reduced and diving becomes dangerous; so when choosing the time for a holiday to an island it is advisable to go when the monsoon is not blowing.

The northern end of the Red Sea is virtually land locked and not subject to the long fetch of open sea where large waves build up. The sea in this area is

If you learn to dive on holiday you will usually attract an interested audience.

A fantastic coral seascape awaits the diver who can travel to the seas where the trade winds blow.

Above *this bronze statue of* Christ of the Abyss *is visited by thousands of divers every year. It stands in the John Pennekamp Coral Reef State Park in Florida.* Below *diving in the warm clear tideless waters of the Florida Keys is far less taxing than diving off the Cornish Coast, but instructor Roger still keeps a wary eye on a novice diver.*

good for diving all year round. Along much of the coast the drop off is close to the shore and can easily be reached from the beach without a boat.

If money is no obstacle the opportunities for a diving holiday are enormous. The Caribbean, Indian Ocean, Red Sea, China Sea, Great Barrier Reef, Galapagos, Honduras, Mauritius and a host of other names spring to mind. When going to such exotic parts of the globe, however, the traveller relies heavily on the advice from his travel agent. Unfortunately many travel agents know little about diving or the diving facilities that various centres have to offer. Look very carefully at the details of package holidays — particularly those offering very cheap holidays to exotic places. The cost of hiring equipment and going for a dive may be quite expensive. All-inclusive holidays may, therefore, be more economical than apparently much cheaper holidays which offer only demi-pension and exclude diving costs.

Holiday diving centres

At holiday diving centres in areas where the sea is warm, clear and tideless it is possible for any reasonably fit person, regardless of age, to dive safely and enjoy the beauty of the underwater world with the minimum of tuition. Some diving centres are geared to give holiday makers who have never

dived before, and who may never dive again, the unique opportunity to sample the underwater world under the watchful eye of a qualified instructor.

There is another type of diver, however, who wants to become seriously involved with diving but who does not have the time to go through the protracted training, with the weekly attendance at a swimming pool, required by many clubs. These busy people can be trained at a holiday diving centre. It is usual for such schools to insist on a doctor's certificate stating that the pupil is suitably fit before training begins.

In most diving centres the standard of tuition is beyond reproach. Diving schools that are permitted to award certificates recognised by diving bodies of international repute, such as CMAS, BSAC and NAUI, (National Association of Underwater Instructors) train their pupils to specified levels of competence. The pupils must attend all the lectures and pass all the practical tests before they are awarded their certificates. Pupils who do not pass the tests do not get certificates.

However, diving schools are in business to make money. Some unscrupulous operators award impressive looking certificates regardless of diving ability. This has led to the discredit of some certificates and to a general suspicion of all diving qualifications except those awarded by well

Members of an underwater safari led by the author, are photographed with their cameras.

established schools or internationally recognised organisations.

If you decide to become a certified diver it is advisable to choose a holiday centre that has been authorised to award certificates (such as the CMAS star certificates) that you can use should you travel to other parts of the world. It is of course entirely in your own interests to be competent in all of the tests. If you can automatically deal with emergency situations then you are not going to a liability to yourself, or anyone else. That is why many diving centres require you to produce a certificate before they will hire out equipment to you, or let you accompany a dive. They want to be sure that you will come back safely.

A comprehensive guide to underwater holidays can be obtained from Twickenham Travel, 22 Church Street, Twickenham.

Ashley Dobbs went on his first sea dive off the Island of Elba in the Mediterranean when he was aged eleven. Children under the age of sixteen should not dive with an aqualung unless their parents are experienced divers who fully understand the risks involved.

This fishing net can easily be seen in the clear water off the Island of Elba. In the murky waters off the British coast it is possible for divers to swim into a fouled net, so they should always carry knives in case they have to cut themselves free.

Turning Professional

It has often been said that the happiest people are those whose hobby becomes their job. Most professional divers are in this category. They took up skindiving as a sport, were captivated by it, and then looked for ways of making their living as professionals. The term 'professional diver' could be applied to a number of people. It could be applied to the person who earns his living as an instructor at a holiday diving centre. However, it is generally understood that 'pro divers' — as they call themselves — are those whose jobs involve working underwater whilst wearing diving apparatus. The demand for such men has increased rapidly in recent years, due partly to the discovery of gas and oil in the North Sea. New technology in the oil industry has created a demand for intelligent divers with technical skills in addition to their ability to work underwater. The oil companies employ some of their own divers, but most of the underwater work is contracted out to specialist companies who provide divers from among their employees.

Professional diving in the North Sea is still a highly hazardous business. So turning 'pro' is not a decision to be taken lightly.

I recently asked a manager of one of the world's biggest employers of professional divers, Comex, what he looked for when he recruited new trainee divers for his company. His reply was simple: 'experience'. He said that he would far rather take on a diver who had reached a high level of proficiency in sports diving than someone, without experience, who just thought that he would like to be a professional diver. Training divers in deep diving is expensive, and despite very careful selection, there is a high fall-out rate in all professional diver training schemes. It is sound economic sense, as well as being in the best interests of the trainees, to keep the success rate as high as possible. An experienced amateur has a far better idea of what is expected of him than a raw recruit who has never been underwater.

The gap between the amateur and the professional can only be bridged with a course of training by professional divers. The type of tuition available to the aspiring recruit is extremely varied. In addition to training their own staff, some professional diving companies offer short courses on 'pro' diving as one of their services. There are also diving schools whose sole function is to train divers.

The first stage in training is to become a 'compressed air diver'. Compressed air is used for relatively shallow work, usually to a maximum depth of 50 metres; and the diver is instructed in the use of the apparatus that supplies a diver with ordinary air under pressure. He will, of course, practise using the equipment in the water, often in a training tank. In addition he is likely to be taught underwater cutting, welding and the use of underwater explosives. Having completed his training on compressed air the diver will be expected to gain professional experience before progressing to the next stage in training, which will enable him to descend well beyond the depth of 50 metres. To do this he will need to breathe a mixture of oxygen and helium and move into an altogether more sophisticated realm of diving requiring extremely expensive back-up facilities.

A course at one of the recently approved professional diving schools in Britain may last for 12 weeks and cost about £2,000. The diver may either pay this fee out of his own pocket, or be sponsored by one of the professional diving companies. Alternatively, he can go to the Government for aid. The Government run a scheme known as TOPS (Training Opportunities Scheme) which was set up to help mature people train for new jobs. Details of the scheme can be obtained from your local Employment Services Agency. The successful applicant in this scheme has his fees, his accommodation and other benefits met out of the national purse.

Once he is trained and gained experience opportunities for employment exist in all of the oceans of the world.

This is a far far cry from where we started in this book: having fun snorkelling round the rocks with equipment costing only a few pounds. But that's how skindiving affects some people. They become addicts, and end up as 'pro divers' making their livelihoods on the sea bed.

Escape into a divers' paradise: the clear waters of the Red Sea.